Love Letters from Exes

Proof That Life Goes On After a Breakup and Love Is What You Make it

Original Edition

SAGE WILCOX

Love Letters from Exes: Proof That Life Goes On After a Breakup and Love Is What You Make It

Copyright © 2016 Sage Wilcox

First Edition, 2016

ISBN-13: 978-0-9849322-9-0

ISBN-10: 0-9849322-9-1

Library of Congress Control Number: 2016938200

Printed in the United States of America.

DEDICATION

To all of my exes, and to all of yours too. Thank you for all you've taught us. I trust that we are right where we are supposed to be. There's no need to look back or wonder what might have been, because if we were meant to be together, well then, that's where we'd be.

"Someday, everything will make perfect sense. So for now, laugh at the confusion, smile through the tears, be strong and keep reminding yourself that everything happens for a reason." ~ Unknown

TABLE OF CONTENTS

WITH GRATITUDE

Deepest thanks to those who shared their heartfelt letters, stories, and insights. I am touched and honored to work with you. Through your experiences, you have shown others that they are not alone. And that with faith, perseverance, and hope, love is a realistic goal that is attainable.

Many thanks to my family and friends for their sincere love and support; I can feel it, and it is greatly appreciated. My life is full and abundant and full of love because of you.

Deep, humble appreciation goes to the Divine Source; my Great Creator, in whom I aspire to grow closer to every day, with great faith.

And thanks to those who decided to pick up this book. I hope you find something inside that resonates with you. Let's pour our favorite drink, find a comfortable spot, and get started, shall we?

PREFACE

When my best friend called me completely distraught because her teenage daughter was suffering a break-up, my first reaction was that it's no big deal. But then I got to thinking. My first heartbreak occurred when I was 16 years old. Shawn was the first boy I truly loved, or so I thought. I knew that we would be together forever. Shawn was all that I thought about, day and night, and night and day, and in every space in between. My mom thought I was silly, but she had been single since I was four years old, so what did she know about love, really? That's how I felt anyway. My dad, on the other hand, was cool with it - but he lived over three hours away from me, and I only saw him a few times a year during school vacations and such, so what choice did he have? Some would say this is why I fell so hard for this boy - because I didn't have a male figure in my daily life, showing me love and affection on a regular basis. Who knows, all I knew at the time was that Shawn was all that I had ever dreamed of; tall, dark, and handsome. He was extremely cute, outgoing, confident, funny, and a good kisser. I couldn't take my eyes off of him. Everyone at school referred to him by a nickname; the name of a popular Hollywood heartthrob -because that's just how gorgeous he was.

He was the first boy who invited me to his house for dinner. We rode the bus after-school to his house, on a warm summer day. As I handed the large, sweaty bus-driver the note my mom had written; giving me permission, I feared that he would think I had forged it and not allow me on the bus. It seemed like it was taking him forever to read the note. My fear was unfounded and I followed Shawn to the back of the bus, where he took my backpack and allowed me to slip into the seat first. Immediately after we sat down, he held my hand. He looked into my eyes, smiled a gorgeous smile and asked with genuine concern "How are you doing?" My heart raced I was so happy! "Great." I excitedly replied. He wore a tight white t-shirt with even tighter button-fly jeans. I weighed about 100 pounds and felt tiny sitting next to him. He had strong thighs – they looked huge in his skin tight jeans. He was definitely all boy, and I loved being next to him. The other kids on the bus kept looking back at us, and I couldn't help but feel proud to be Shawn's guest that day.

Shawn's home was beautiful; and looked like an old mansion. His father and step-mother were both polite. As we sat down for dinner Shawn scooped some mashed potatoes and placed a few slices of ham onto my plate for me. After dinner, we went to his bedroom. It was on the third floor and around a back corner, and it appeared to be part of a huge attic. It was all wood, ceiling to floor, with minimal lighting. We laughed and kissed as we lay on his bed.

My after-school visits became a regular routine and we'd always end up in Shawn's bedroom. I was shy and inexperienced – something I now realize every 16-year-old girl should be – but it got pretty hot and heavy at times. Shawn never pressured me, but the more intense it got; the more intensely I loved him it seemed. Every time we'd leave his room, we'd have to straighten out our clothes, and smooth down our hair. The more petting we did, the more my mind was consumed with him. And the more I dreamed of him. And the more I loved him.

I was content with kissing and touching Shawn and that was good for me. I knew he wasn't a virgin, but I was too scared to do anything else – not scared of him in any way – I just wasn't ready and I listened to that inner guidance... for a little while anyway.

I was completely happy with our relationship until Shawn started becoming distant. He wasn't calling as much, didn't invite me over as often, and I felt confused. This went on for weeks until one day I decided I'd just call him so that I could talk to him about it. (This was before call-waiting, and cell phones.) As I anxiously waited for someone to pick up, I got a busy signal instead. I tried for 30 minutes straight, and it was still busy so I figured I'd vent to one of my best friends, who also happened to be my next-door neighbor. As I dialed Paula's number, I was so ready to burst into tears. I didn't know why Shawn was acting this way. Oddly enough, Paula's phone number was busy as well. Both numbers continued to be busy for another hour. And yeah, you guessed it. Shawn and Paula started liking each other. Paula was two years older than me... and popular... and pretty... and a varsity cheerleader... and *not* a virgin.

When Shawn started picking Paula up for school in the mornings, they'd pass me by at the bus stop, and it was almost unbearable. I was sure they were having sex and wondered if maybe I shouldn't have said no to him all of those times. Maybe he would've stayed with me. Maybe I should've been braver. I mean, I had friends who were younger than me who were having sex. If they could do it, so could I!

I cried for two weeks straight; seriously. Add in my screaming "I f*cking hate you!" at the tops of my lungs as they drove by me at the bus stop. And running down the road to another friend's house where I collapsed on her front lawn sobbing. Now, as an adult, I can't even imagine what my friend's parents must have thought at the time. Severe drama queen, maybe.

Man, if I had known then what I know now.

If I had known then, what I know now, I would've said "Good riddance. I'm not ready, and if you can't wait and want to date someone else, I cannot stop you. Obviously, we are not meant to be together because I want to be with someone who loves me enough to be patient. I harbor no ill feelings towards you and appreciate this opportunity to see your true colors."

Paula and I are still good friends, after all of these years – 28 to be exact. She's awesome and I love her tons.

As for Paula and Shawn, they broke up about six months later; an eternity for some high school relationships. As for Shawn and me, the story did not end there.

I don't remember a lot of the details – a blessing I've always been fortunate enough to possess – my long-term memory just doesn't contain many details. I do remember, though, that while Shawn and Paula were together, I pretended to be happy for them. I'd visit them both at her house - sounds messed up I know - but I just wanted to be near him. I decided to take up running and I always tried to time it so that I was outside as Shawn was driving in, or out, of Paula's driveway. Often times, when I timed it just right, he would stop and chat for a few minutes. YES! Victory! Or so it seemed at the time.

I watched them go to prom, occasionally caught a ride to school with them, and always acted like it was no big deal to have my best friend date my first love.

When they broke up, I pretended to be sad for them. By this time, I was 17, had my license, and was allowed to go on dates without parental supervision. Paula went off to college, and Shawn and I started talking and hanging out again.

Shawn apologized and was extremely sweet. He told me that he had sometimes wished he had never broken up with me. He took me places and brought me to meet more of his family. He even surprised me with dozens of roses in my locker, and once again I was very happy.

If I had known then, what I know now, I would've known that my happiness didn't depend on Shawn or dozens of roses. But that I could create my own happiness! And that happiness truly does come from within.

Shawn started coming over more often, and I'd tell my mom that we were going into town to get a bite to eat. Instead, we'd take a left-hand turn down a long dirt road, which connected to another dirt road, which connected to another dirt road, which was also known as "The Sand Pit". Shawn would park his car and we'd hop in the back and talk, kiss, laugh, and touch each other.

One day Shawn picked me up in his little, blue Ford Escort. As we drove down the road, a big grin came across his gorgeous face and he grabbed my hand. He looked at me with his big brown eyes and said, "Tonight's *the* night. You're going to be completely mine tonight, finally."

A bit surprised, but in total agreement, I gushingly replied

"Really?!"

"Yes. Really."

I placed my hand on his knee and leaned over and nuzzled into his neck. I kissed his earlobe and cheek in approval.

Shawn took me to a quiet and private place. He led me around a corner, up a wide stairwell, and into a dark room that was modernly furnished. He closed the door behind him, pulled me close and started slowly kissing my neck.

"I don't want to waste any more time." He whispered. "I want to make sure that you're okay with this, though." He lightly kissed my bottom lip as he spoke. "I've been kissing these lips for over a year now, and I know that you love me."

I took a deep breath, as his hand moved along the inside of the back of my shirt. "Yes, I do love you." I rested my hands into his back pockets.

"Do you love me?" I asked.

"You know that I do," Shawn replied looking into my eyes.

If I had known then, what I know now, I would've known that you shouldn't have to ask someone if they love you. I would've known that love doesn't question. That love doesn't break-up with you for your best-friend. That love doesn't hurt. That love doesn't rush. That you need to love yourself before you can love someone else. And that with self-love comes self-respect. I would've known that when you love and respect yourself, you don't give yourself away so easily.

Shawn backed up slowly, towards a big leather mahogany

chair that sat almost in the center of the room. He sat down with me still facing him and placed his hands on my hips.

"You're so innocent." He said. "It's one of the things I love about you. It'll be okay. Just trust me. I won't hurt you, I promise."

And from there we proceeded to finally make "tonight *the* night".

Shawn was extremely patient and gentle, but it didn't really work. I guess it *kind of* worked, but not really. Either way, it was a moment that I'll remember forever. I felt wanted. I loved being close to him. I loved holding his hand. I loved being in his arms. Those moments made me feel loved. It felt nice, and I was willing to do whatever it took, to continue to feel that "love".

As Shawn drove me home and kissed me goodnight, he said that it would get easier and better as time went on, and he was right. For more than a year, we spent 'time' together.

But the heartache that came after our 'time' together was even harder than the first time we broke up. I could not understand it, and neither did my heart. Shawn became interested in another girl in my class; someone who was pretty and athletic. I felt like I wasn't good enough. I wished I was a different person. I wished I was more athletic. I wished I didn't have to work full-time while going to school so that I could play sports. I wished I was prettier. I cried, off and on, for months this time around and I didn't want to talk to anyone. My mom tried to console me, but nothing she did helped, and I didn't even want her to try. My friends tried to set me up with other guys, but I couldn't even consider dating anyone other than Shawn. If I saw him in the hall at school, I'd drop my head and act like a sad little puppy dog. I had hoped that if he saw how unhappy I was, he'd change his mind, and take me back.

If I'd known then what I know now, I'd realize just how silly that tactic was; acting like a sad little puppy-dog, would make anyone want to run in the opposite direction. If I'd known then what I know now, I would've known that I'm perfect just the way I am. That everyone has individual strengths and weaknesses, and that's what makes us all special in our own way. I would've known that I was good enough, and that Shawn didn't deserve my innocence. I would've taken full responsibility for my actions. I wouldn't have given myself to him so freely. I would've known that both of us had basically been 'thrown to the wolves' in regards to romantic relationships. We were not taught, nor had we witnessed, how to maintain a loving, respectful relationship.

At the time, I wish I would've had some guidance, some knowledge in regards to relationships; some self-esteem would've been nice as well. Little did I know, I possessed all of those qualities within... they were just buried deep, deep, deep down inside.

My sad, pathetic, head hung low, puppy-dog look, did not change Shawn's mind. He had moved on to another girl in my class, and he no longer wanted anything to do with me. Shawn's new girl appeared to be everything I wasn't. She was everything I didn't think I was. Confident, strong, secure. I had given myself to someone who didn't really love me. And if I had really loved myself, I would've seen that beforehand.

If I'd known then what I know now, I would've realized that I was confident, strong, and secure enough and that I was perfect just the way I was. I would've loved myself; therefore, I would've recognized all of the minor little details that were clear evidence that this person wasn't coming from a place of love for me. And I would've also realized that it wasn't his fault. He only knew what he had learned from his divorced parents. We thought we loved each other, but neither one of us had been taught the real meaning of love...

As time went on, and through many more life experiences, I learned and grew and matured. I started to slowly learn The Word. I read my Bible more and more with each year that passed. The Bible contains 66 different books and was written over a period of roughly 2,000 years by 40 different authors from three different continents, who wrote in three different languages. The wisdom I have gained from this historical book has been absolutely amazing; it's been a freedom like no other.

I'm finding that the most important information, contained in the 129 self-help books that I own, and crowd my bookshelves, has already been covered and addressed in this one book; the Bible.

The advice, most given, is to love one another. It's a pretty simple concept. No matter what the age or circumstances, love is powerful. It can redeem, or it can destroy... or so we think. Can love really destroy? No, love cannot destroy. Love is patient and kind. Love trusts, and values. Love forgives, and heals. Love supports, and encourages. Love is always selfless, respectful and giving. Always. Love would never destroy anything.

Experts say we are either coming from love or fear. I believe this to be true. The ego wants you to come from fear, pride, selfishness, arrogance, competition, and the like. But love never blames or asks "What's in this for me?" Our inner-being always want us to come from a place of love; to love the Divine Source, yourself, and others as one in the same.

This first heartache of mine was in 1987. 1987! Oh, how times have changed. Teenagers nowadays are faced with a whole myriad of new troubles, challenges, and struggles. The internet (and porn in particular) is ruining relationships more than ever before. And a high percentage of teens haven't been taught the skills needed to overcome such unhealthy circumstances and atrocities; that, unfortunately, are available at their fingertips. Porn is clearly not an accurate depiction of how sexual relationships should be, and experts are finding that young boys are being desensitized; therefore, they are having a hard time connecting and being truly satisfied and fulfilled by real love experiences with others. Young boys and girls, who have been exposed to inappropriate and unhealthy internet sites, are left feeling empty and alone.

So how can we ease the heartaches? How can we help others? How can we help ourselves? How can we help our daughters and our sons, our granddaughters, and our grandsons for generations to come? How can we teach the characteristics that make up a good person? How can we raise children to have good morals and high standards? How can we raise our children, to be honest, trustworthy, and responsible? We can learn. We can research. We can become vigilant. We can teach and pass this wisdom along. We can look out for each another. And we can *LOVE* one another. Not with a false, and selfish love, but with true and genuine love. The real meaning of love; not the definition of love we have made up, and adjusted to meet our own needs, but real love.

When you find yourself feeling any negative feelings towards a person you love, for example, jealousness, enviousness, rudeness, competition, blame, insecurity, doubt, or even expectation, know that you are not coming from a place of love. If you feel headed in the direction of one of those negative feelings, just stop, be aware of what you are feeling, and deliberately move in the direction of love instead.

Recite what love really is, if you'd like, to remind yourself. Look it up: 1 Corinthians 13:4-7

Love is what you make it, and it's meant to be wonderful. Love is always patient. Love is always kind. Love is always trusting. Love is always giving without expecting anything in return. Love is Heaven on Earth. Love is amazing!

When people are asked to name a time in their lives when they felt the happiest and healthiest, most say it was when they first fell in love. And when you truly understand love, you can learn that you can easily re-create that first-love feeling anytime you want. Love is exciting. Love is rewarding. Love is healing. Love can change the world for the better. It's time to step-up to the plate. It's time to take responsibility. It's time to take action. It's time to move in a deliberate direction. It's time to love like never before!

When we love, we learn to forgive. We forgive those who hurt us. And we forgive those who decide they no longer want to be with us. It's a hard concept at first, but when you learn to trust the Divine Source and its timing, you learn to go with the flow and know that something better must be coming your way.

All things work together for your good. Get ready. Good things are coming your way!

SAGE WILCOX

*"This is why we call people exes, I guess –
because the paths that cross in the middle
end up separating at the end. It's too easy to
see an X as a cross-out. It's not, because
there's no way to cross out something like
that. The X is a diagram of two paths."*
~ John Green

ABOUT THIS BOOK

This is not just a book about breakups, heartache, and common words of everlasting love. And it is not just a book about people who change their minds after promising forever.

This is a book of hope; a book about young and old love, a book about growth, change and so much more. It's about self-worth, self-confidence, and self-love. And, yes, it's even about forgiveness. It's a book about lessons learned, moving forward, and becoming better people. This book is meant for all who desire true love that lasts.

You will find over 30 love letters that were written while the recipient and the sender were together You will also find, in the *Love Insights* section, deep confessions of lessons learned. And, thankfully, we can learn from other people's experiences.

Breakups are often described as a "death" of sorts. The grief that comes with a breakup can be unbearable, and extremely hard to understand. Whether it's a high-school breakup, a long-term relationship, or a 25-year marriage; hearts break regardless.

Coping with a breakup can be one of the biggest challenges one can face in life, and one most are unprepared to face. Dreams are shattered, hearts are broken, and, at first, it can feel like there's no hope whatsoever. Confusion, disappointment, and deep insecurities set in when we are told we are no longer needed, wanted, or loved.

But as hard as it seems in those moments, breakups are not the end of the world, and this book is proof of that.

This first part of this book is full of genuine, heartfelt love letters... You will be moved by the deep, emotional honesty contained in these letters. These particular relationships did not work out; people's hearts were broken, people changed their minds, people made mistakes, but each and every one of these people survived. They eventually picked up the pieces, in their own time, and moved forward. They didn't give up on love and were determined to do better in love the next time. And they learned valuable lessons, gaining wisdom and knowledge, they wouldn't have otherwise. Some of the letters are shorter than others, some deeper than others, but each contains individual expressions of hope and love.

The second part of the book is filled with ideas and tools on creating the love that you truly desire. Love is what you make it! Just like riding a bike, once you learn how, if you keep at it, it will become easier and easier to maintain your balance and succeed.

Whether you are currently going through a break-up, or you've been married for 40 years, this book can inspire you and encourage you to make loving changes for the better.

You will gain insight on how to love yourself, so you can truly love another.

Filled with inspiring and fitting quotes, this book and the love letters and wisdom shared within will bring comfort to those who have suffered a break-up or divorce; and encourage those who are in relationships to improve and enhance their current love-lives.

May this book be a gentle reminder that love is the greatest gift, and that it's more attainable and rewarding than you know. Love is a choice, and everyone should be madly in love! May you be blessed with peace and comfort, and lots of love.

Love Letters from Exes

*Proof That Life Goes On After a Breakup
and Love Is What You Make It*

"In this sad world of ours, sorrow comes to all...It comes with bitterest agony...Perfect relief is not possible, except with time. You cannot now realize that you will ever feel better...And yet this is a mistake. You are sure to be happy again. To know this, which is certainly true, will make you some less miserable now. I have experienced enough to know what I say."
~ Abraham Lincoln

Love Letter 1

Dear Sue,

As I'm sitting here trying to stop thinking about you long enough to get some work done, I figured I'd just tell you what I'm thinking...maybe that will clear my mind.

I am completely shocked and amazed that I have fallen for you so hard and so fast.... not because of the amazing person you are but because I've never done it before. I am in love with every part of you.... mind, body, and soul. You are everything a man could ask for.... smart, funny, beautiful, sexy, kind, caring, passionate, honest, giving...but most of all, you "get it." You get that a real relationship is about finding someone that you can open up to and learn from and teach and grow with; someone that you can let your guard down with and know that they would never hurt you. Someone that you can commit to 100% and feel safe with knowing that they are giving their all to you. I am so happy that the few "tests" we've had haven't just gone well, they've been perfect.

I think we're doing awesome with it and you deserve most of the credit for that. I don't expect to see you every time before or after work. I know sometimes you're going to have other things to do or you're just going to want to go home at a decent time and I hope you never feel obligated to see me. I'm trying to stay realistic and remember that things will happen when the time is right, but I cannot help thinking about the life we're going to make together. I want to protect you and take care of you and make you laugh and put my arms around you every night.

If this doesn't freak you out and send you running, I don't think anything will!! And that's fine with me!

I love you!!!

Jeff

"One makes mistakes; that is life. But it is never a mistake to have loved."
~ Romain Rolland

Love Letter 2

Dear Rhett,

I miss you so much. Thank you for being you, and for loving me. When your strong arms are around me I feel so safe and secure; like I don't have a care in the world. All stressful thoughts just melt away.

I'm lying on my bed, thinking of you, and looking at a few of the pictures Lisa took of us, from that night at the dance club. I love looking at them.

In one of the photos, you are standing behind me; your right hand is protectively resting on my hip, and your left arm is wrapped around the front of me, pulling me as close to you as possible. Your hand is slightly up under the edge of my shirt, resting on my belly-button. My hand is perfectly placed on the top of yours and your mouth is very close to my ear. You have the most content look on your face; like there is no place on earth that you'd rather be. The camera captured your mood perfectly, and the look on your face makes me feel... special, I guess. Anyway, I like it! The other photo is of us kissing, our lips fitting perfectly together, and you have this look of immense hunger. Like you wish we were alone in that moment. It's cute and sexy, and it makes me wish you were here right now!

I also love how we have our song and we know that no matter what we are doing, or who we are talking to; everything stops in that moment. It's our song, and we always drop what we are doing and find each other immediately. It makes me smile to think about it. When they play our song, I know, that you know, that I am looking for you. There is nothing or no one who could come between us during our song. And when we finally find each other, in the sea of people, you lead me to the dance floor, put your arms possessively around me to let others know that I am yours, lightly brush your lips against my neck and whisper the lyrics of love in my ear. Until our lips meet that is. My heart starts beating faster and my breathing gets shallow. You kiss me so softly, yet so passionately. It feels like it's just me and you out there. I also love how you let me untuck the back of your shirt so that I can rub my hands up your strong, bare back. You're so good to me. ☺

You're the first man to open my car door for me (on a regular basis), and I love how you smile down at me as you gently close the door behind me. Your sweet smile always makes me feel like the luckiest woman in the world. You're the first man to always pull out my chair before I sit down, and help push it in before you sit down yourself. Such simple gestures but they make me feel incredibly loved and cared for. Respected, cherished, adored...

Sometimes I feel confused about this crazy life we live in, but when I'm in your presence, the craziness just fades away.

I love how you own properties, and invest, and have your retirement plan already figured out. You've got your shit together and it impresses the shit out of me. Haha! Seriously, though!

I know your job is a dangerous one, but for some reason, I'm not worried about you. I know how courageous, and strong, and smart you are.

I guess I just want to thank you. I hope you know how grateful I am for you. You make me feel like no one else ever has.

I love how whenever I call, you are always there for me. Sometimes my life can get so crazy, but it doesn't matter when or what time I call you, you always pick up. I ask, "Can I come over?" and you always answer, "Definitely, please do."

When I get to your place, and you open your front door for me, the only place I want to be is in your arms. And I appreciate that we stay that way for quite some time, standing in the middle of your kitchen, just holding and kissing each other. I love how you touch and caress me all over in those first moments. It's amazing really; having your hands all over me after having been away from you, as you whisper softly "I just want to feel you" in my ear. Mmmmm, you know what you're doing.

Thanks for sharing your toothbrush with me! If that's not love, I don't know what is. ☺

I still can't believe that you use to go running by my apartment! I wish I had known! So I could watch you out the window! Haha! It's funny how we met. I remember that night perfectly; turning around in a crowd of people, making small-talk with you, and then finally introducing myself to you.

I have to admit; I love that you openly talk to your co-workers about me. Hearing you say "There she is", or "Yes, this is her, the one I'm always talking about" or "I'd like you to meet Adrianna. Yes, *she's* the one." And when I asked you what would happen if we don't work out long term, you said: "Then I'll regretfully tell people that you're the *one* who got away". It's things like that that I've never experienced before, and it's an incredible feeling.

I'm sorry if I've ever hurt you. It will never be my intention. Sometimes I get scared that I'm not good enough for you, and it's not that you make me feel that way on purpose; it's just internal I guess. But when I feel that way, I feel myself distancing myself from you. It's hard to describe in words.

Oh and the way you end your letters to me, also makes me

feel like never before; 'Anything for you', 'Always yours', 'Yours', or 'Eternally yours'. I close my eyes and absorb your words knowing that you're telling the truth. Maybe one day I'll understand why.

I hope that you know that I'm thinking of you, even when we're not together. And I'm forever thankful for the moments we have already shared. You're like the essentials needed in a storm. Most people run out to buy milk and eggs. I feel as though I just need you, Rhett. You're my essentials. You're my shelter. You make this chaotic word feel calm.

You amaze me. I'm amazed by you. I am inspired by you. I am in awe of you and how you treat me. It's really nice and you're really nice, and I love you. Thanks for all of it. I'm really glad that you're in my life.

Love Always,

Adrianna

"Letting go doesn't mean that you don't care about someone anymore. It's just realizing that the only person you really have control over is yourself."
~ Deborah Reber

Love Letter 3

Dear Ann,

I'm thinking of you today. I really like the way things are going between us and I hope they continue to grow. I'm finding that you're on my mind more often than not and I always smile while thinking of you.

I hope that we can go out again real soon. Spending time with you was a lot of fun and I honestly didn't want the night to end. Hearing you laugh was one of the best parts of the night and I am looking forward to many more nights like that with YOU. I hope you feel the same.

Thinking of you,

Doug

"Watching you walk out of my life does not make me bitter or cynical about love. But rather makes me realize that if I wanted so much to be with the wrong person how beautiful it will be when the right one comes along."
~ Unknown

Love Letter 4

Dear Ann,

Congratulations on your job promotion. You've worked hard and you deserve it. I know you will be in the area for another year anyway, and then you'll have to decide where you want to go from here. Hopefully, I'll still be there when you do. I think I will. I hope you do too. Ann, we have a really great thing going and I would never screw it up. You can trust me on that one.

I will do whatever it takes to make it work with you. Now that you're in my life, I can't imagine it being any other way.

I loved rubbing your hair while you fell asleep in my arms last night. After I covered you up and left, I found myself smiling on my way home at the thought of how beautiful you were as you slept soundly.

Now don't go thinking you're better than me now just because you've got the world in the palm of your hands. You wouldn't dare to anyway. Haha. Just kidding. You're amazing and I know you'll succeed at all that you do.

Fondly and lovingly,

Doug

"After a breakup, it takes a couple weeks for the fog to settle, but it's always a period of self-priority and growth."
~ Brittany Murphy

LOVE LETTERS FROM EXES

Love Letter 5

Dear Ann,

Hi, baby! It's such a lovely day today isn't it? You look so beautiful and sexy in your new outfit today. It's been a challenge to look at you without going crazy.

Have I told you lately that I love you? Probably I have, but remember that means much more than just those three words. And I love you very much. My feelings are very strong for you. I don't want to see us break-up ever. Although I hate to think about it, you are probably right, we might not be together forever, but I hope we stay together for a long time anyway. I love being around you. You are always so cheery and happy. I love cooking with you. I love watching football with you. I love playing Skip-Bo with you. I even love cleaning with you! And I can't imagine not being with you.

Your card was very special. It's like we feel the exact same way. We never fight, and we are always laughing when we are together. You're everything I could want and more. Do not forget it baby. It's like I've found the missing link in my life. YOU! Days are so much brighter with you in my arms.

I love you very much and always will,

Doug

"Getting over a painful experience is much like crossing monkey bars. You have to let go at some point in order to move forward."
~ Unknown

Love Letter 6

Ann,

Hi, baby! How are you doing sex goddess? I'm great, but just a little tired because you kept me up all night. I didn't mind, though, really I loved it. And I love you, and I promise to love you forever.

I suppose we can go shopping tonight, as long as you don't take two hours to pick something out. If I say buy something, you buy it. That includes kinky underwear and sexy nightgowns. Haha.

I'd love to spend the night with you tonight, but if you don't want me to, I'll understand. I'll still come over to see you, though.

You look so beautiful and sexy in my shirt today. I feel like laying you down right on the sidewalk when I'm around you... but then everyone would gather around in a circle and want to watch us. Haha.

You mentioned going running tonight. I don't know if I will feel up to it or not. Also, I would hate to embarrass you by leaving you to eat my dust. Haha

So, yes we can go shopping if you'd like. You know I don't really like to go shopping, but I'll go for you. Just because I love you so much, and I always will.

Love always,

Doug

"If you break up with your partner, go straight to the studio. You're going to make great music."
~ B.o.B.

Love Letter 7

To my dearest Ann,

Hi, my love. How are you? Let me answer that for you. You're fine! You're mighty fine indeed! I'm doing great and just want you to know that I'm thinking about you and I want to say Happy Anniversary! I love you so much honey and I always will, too. I promise.

We get along so well. You're my best friend and I love you more each and every day.

Love always and forever,

Doug

"He loved me. He loved me, but he doesn't love me anymore, and it's not the end of the world."
~Jennifer Weiner

Love Letter 8

Dear Ann,

Hi, how are you today? I'm great because I had a very good weekend with you. Wow, it was amazing, and I loved every single minute of it. It was the best getting a little crazy!

We also had some good talks and it seemed like we were really close. I had a good time playing football with you yesterday as well. You're a great football player! Haha! And you looked striking in my football jersey. My shins are still killing me from making that catch while jumping over the rear-end of that car.

Well, you're the best honey. Thanks for all that you do. Thanks for helping me finish that project for work. I don't know what I'd do without you and if you want to take me to dinner tonight, I won't refuse. Haha.

I love you with all of my heart and I always will. I promise. You have nothing to even think about when it comes to my love.

Love you honey,

Doug

"We must be willing to let go of the life we've planned, so as to have the life that is waiting for us."
~ Joseph Campbell

Love Letter 9

Dear Ann, <u>my one, and only true love,</u>

I hope this gift will make you laugh a little bit, because when you are smiling and laughing it makes you even more beautiful than you already are.

Although I can't give you much more than this little gift, I wish I could give you anything you ever wished for in your life. One thing is for sure, you will always have my love. We have an amazing relationship and I hope it never ends.

I love you more than anything else on earth Ann! I know it's hard for you to trust me now, but you can trust me with anything. Believe me Ann! Let's be together forever!

I'm sorry about what happened a few days ago. If you know what I was thinking at the time, you would've known I didn't really mean that we should take a break. I don't ever want to be without you! I love you so much and I know I always will.

As I think back, I think of how our love has grown. I'll do

all that I can to build on our love. You add so much beauty to all of my days and I've found such happiness with you. I love sharing my hopes, plans, and dreams with you. Thanks for being so patient with me. If you only knew how much it means, and how truly important you are to me.

I LOVE YOU FOREVER AND ALWAYS,

Your honey forever,

Doug

---

*"The brightest future will always be based
on a forgotten past, you can't go on well in
life until you let go of your past failures and
heartaches."*
~ Anonymous

Love Letter 10

Dear Bill,

Happy birthday to the most important man in my life; you have lifted my happiness to a level I only thought existed in other people's lives. I always knew it was possible, but didn't think I'd ever get to taste it for myself. You and your love have changed all of that for me.

I know I have told you all of this before, but I will never get tired of telling you how much I love you and how much I care about you and how much joy you add to my life. I love waking up with you every single morning and I love going to sleep with you every single evening. Your skin is like a security blanket that makes everything okay.

I will never get tired of remembering our first night together. Thinking of those moments with you makes me warm inside. They make my heart sing. Those great memories bring a smile to my face and bring me comfort. Now I know why those moments felt so right. We are meant to be together.

I want to love you like you've never been loved before and I want to make you feel like the most important person in the world because, in my world, that is what you are.

Thank you for being an amazing person. Thank you for always respecting my feelings. Thank you for always listening to me. Thank you for loving me. I love you for you and I look forward to many more happy moments with you.

I will always be here for you. You will never have to doubt my love for you.

I love you sincerely and always.

Mary

"When we are in love, we are convinced nobody else will do. But as time goes, others do do, and often do do, much much better."
~ Coco J. Ginger

Love Letter 11

Dear Jane,

I hope that a single rose hasn't been outdated by today's standards.

I had a great time talking with you last night. I can't believe how much we have in common. After you left I was thinking of the first night I saw you. I was sitting at that table outside the restaurant and you and Sherri walked up behind me. When I turned and saw you, I couldn't believe how pretty you are. I almost had to scrape my tongue out of the sand. You have a real natural beauty, Jane. You don't have to get all made up to be beautiful. That kind of beauty is hard to come by and even harder to find attached to such a wonderful person.

Jane, I realize we haven't known each other for very long, but as a counselor, it is my job to know people and you are a very special person. You are very kind, fun, not materialistic, you like to play, and be held, and you have a really good head on your shoulders. You have a very good grasp on life from what you've been through.

And on top of all of that, I have never been with a woman and felt like you made me feel that night. Jane, I want you to understand that you are a very beautiful, special person who should be treated as such. I just don't want you to feel that I am out to get as much as I can before I go back to college. In the short time that we've known one another, there is no way I could leave this town and not see you again.

Well, Jane, I'm kind of bummed that I won't see you for four days when I'm in Virginia. But I'll be back soon!

I'm not sure what I've said, but I want you to know that; that rose's beauty is only matched by the woman holding it and that woman is special to me in so many ways. She's so fun to be around, very intelligent, and sexy.

Been thinking of you,

Ben

"Some think love can be measured by the amount of butterflies in their tummy. Others think love can be measured in bunches of flowers, or by using the words 'forever.' But love can only truly be measured by actions. It can be a small thing, such as peeling an orange for a person you love because you know they don't like doing it."
~ Marian Keyes

Love Letter 12

Hi Jane,

I am really sorry that I haven't written sooner. Things have been crazy here. Now that a few months have gone by things will get smoother. I love to write and am a good writer it's just that things have been nuts.....

But now classes start tomorrow and I will be able to have more time to myself. So I will have no excuses for not sending you (the most beautiful woman in the world) letters.

I've been thinking of you so much. I really have even been a little sad about it all; sad because I had to leave. I'm starting to wonder if you realize how hard that was for me. I miss you! I had so much fun with you at the resort. I'd love to spend more time like that. I miss the way we laugh. Lately, I've been working out really hard. I'm getting stronger, but it doesn't look like it's going to change the fact that we're so far apart. That last sentence wasn't too clear. What I meant was I've been working out hard to keep my mind off everything, like missing you and the stress of school.

Jane, I really love to be with you. The time we spent together felt so good and so right. Maybe it was just me, but it really did. You are so beautiful and so smart and so fun to be with and with just those qualities alone you kick the shit out of 90% of the women in this school.

You wouldn't have believed the mess I was in before we met this summer. I don't know it just seems that every relationship I've ever had, something just isn't right. I never once felt that way with you, though. I'm not sure what I'm trying to say. I miss you more than anything, yet I'm afraid to see you because I'm scared it will make it worse. But then again, maybe it would be a lot better. I'm so confused.

I know one thing, though; I can't wait to get your next letter. Hell, you must have a dozen guys after you by now; now that I've gone. Well if they are after you, at least they have great taste in women.

After I get your return letter from this one, be rest assured, my reply will be quick.

Lots of love always, and thinking of you,

Ben

P.S. I miss you.

*"Flatter me, and I may not believe you.
Criticize me, and I may not like you. Ignore
me, and I may not forgive you. Encourage
me, and I will not forget you. Love me and I
may be forced to love you."*
~ William Arthur Ward

Love Letter 13

Dear Jane,

How is everything around you? I hope it's happy. I haven't gotten a return letter from you yet. It is too soon anyway. So here I go writing another letter - because I can't stop thinking about you. My last letter must have confused you a bit. I was confused too. Less confused and more stressed is more like it. The stress is less now, though, and I think I'm getting things under control.

It looks like I may have gotten that job I was telling you about. My files are being reviewed today to find out when they will let me graduate and what I will need to do. This week, I'm going down to the Career Center to start my job search. It would be good to make some money for a change. It's hard for me to believe that all this is going to happen so soon. I will have a lot of opportunities. I'm really excited.

I've also been a bit distracted, though. Not in a bad way. I've been thinking about you so much! That's how I've been distracted. I feel like I'm going crazy without you. Remember when you asked me why I wanted to make love to you the last night we were together? I didn't want you to forget me. I wish you could understand how much I enjoyed being with you. That's why I'm writing this letter. I feel so comfortable with you Jane. I love the things we talk about and I love to hear what you think about things. I must have read the letter I've gotten from you a hundred times; both of them. I read them because it makes me feel like I can, at least, be close to you... somehow.

Jane, you are so pretty and really smart. You would do so well at this university. You have what it takes and so much more. I've never been with anyone like we were that night, and I never shared sunsets and those places with anyone else either. I could stand and watch the stars with you for hours. Jane, I've never felt so close to anyone or so good with anyone like we did in that short period of time. I haven't seen or thought about anyone else like I think of you since we met. I really want to see you again.

I hope I haven't made what we shared this summer into more than it really is. I mean I hope you felt the things I did. If not, I understand. I've really, really missed you and there hasn't been a day that goes by that I haven't thought about you. What do you think of this? I'd really like to see you.

I think now is a good place to stop. I'm starting to make no sense again and its 1 a.m. I've missed you Jane and I haven't been able to stop thinking about the intelligent, beautiful, sexy, and fun to be with woman I met this summer. I'll write again soon. I guess I should wait for one of your letters, though.

Lots of love,

Ben

P.S. I miss you lots.

"*What love we've given,
we'll have forever.
What love we fail to give,
will be lost for all eternity.*"
~ Leo Buscaglia

Love Letter 14

Dear Jane,

You are long overdue this letter. I bet you're even a bit surprised to hear from me. I feel as though there is a lot mixed up. I tried to tell myself that I didn't care, but the fact is I do remember our trip to the resort; the stars, seeing that sunset in the boat and just being with you. Boy, do I miss that.

The distance is what is causing so much pain and confusion I think. Not being able to see you and talk to you face to face. Not being able to hold and kiss you.

I really want to get something cleared up right away. Well, the woman your friends see me eat lunch with in the cafeteria is just a good friend. She has a boyfriend and we've been friends for a long time. We usually eat dinner together.

I know your friends told you that I went on a date with another girl, and you assumed everything was going well for me (that was a sweet letter you wrote by the way). I know we don't have any commitments to each other, but the fact is that I went with that girl as a friend, and I went away to talk all of this mess out. Anyway, to make a long story short, I'm NOT seeing anyone. You have all assumed I am. Your friend doesn't even talk to me anymore because I'm sure she thinks that I am dating the woman I always eat dinner with. She hasn't given me a chance to let her know what's going on. I could have gone over and told her, and I could have written you sooner, but it's been really frustrating. It just seems like I've been pegged as an ass and nobody wants to know the truth about the whole thing. I mean, you people were so close to me. I miss you so much. It's all my fault, though, for pushing you away at the end of the summer. I wish I would have known more of how you felt.

Anyway, it really hasn't been easy for me. School has been very hard and there really hasn't been anybody around. I don't want to make this thing a sob story, though. I recently bought a keyboard and I learned a song for you. It's going along. I am glad I bought it. It's killed a lot of time for me. I'd go out and party but many of my friends have graduated and moved away. My best friend is also moving at the end of this semester. It's all sad, but I didn't write this letter to cry all over the place and to be honest, I'm sick of having wet eyes. I wrote this letter because I've missed you. I know I've sounded really down but I've been keeping busy.

I'm sure by now you've found that man you've been

looking for. He is one lucky man if you have. Have you been looking at schools still? You should! You would do so good and would handle it easy.

I still have that beautiful picture of you in that cool frame. That is such a pretty picture. I picked it up today, looked at it for a long time, and really felt the need to see if I could make you understand. It's been hard being away from you and being so misunderstood.

Well, Jane, I wanted to write and let you know what the real story is. And to tell you that I miss you and I hope to hear from you. If you don't write, I'll understand. At least, I will know that I tried to let you know what has happened.

I miss you and have been thinking of you. I think of the love that we shared. I want that love again. I want that love again with you. And I'm hoping we can find it again.

You always see the positive in everything. You light up every room you enter. Life is drab without you. You make it colorful, wonderful, and fun. You make the darkest days' light, and I long to be with you again. Give me another chance. Let me show you.

Love Always,

Ben

*"Just because a relationship ends, it doesn't
mean it's not worth having."*
~ Sarah Mlynowski

LOVE LETTERS FROM EXES

Love Letter 15

Dear Zoe,

The best thing about this spring day so far has been to see you floating by, snapping your head from side to side, trying to control your smokin' windblown hair. You mesmerize me with your glow that you emit, your constant smile, your body sculpted to perfect proportions. I could almost taste your scent in the air. You are a truly beautiful person, inside and out. You are the definition of ravishing and I am so thankful that I met you so many years ago. I am so happy and fulfilled knowing that we are one. To have you on my arm, and I truly believe this, completes my life.

I know I was never able to put 100% into my previous relationships because when I tried, I found myself changing who I am/was, the thing that I value, the person who I am. I became someone who was just getting by and I suffocated because of it.

You are the focal point that has helped me to realize that

there is life out from under my rock. I want you to understand that you have helped me open my eyes. You are the friend who was sent to help me gain my life back. I can only assume that I was also sent to you to help you for the same reasons. Maybe to help you through a period of time; a situation that you were having that you did not even know was about you.

We are together because we both need each other, different reasons, circumstances, and issues; it is up to us to understand this, work with it and follow what is good for each of us.

I truly believe that you are my soul mate. You make me feel "balanced", complete, whole, finished, pick a word that describes happiness and joy.

You make me happy; I want to grab you, hold you, and love you. You can't buy happiness; happiness is a gift that is given.

How long were you unhappy before we were together? Days, weeks, months, years? Before you, I was blinded, weak and not fully understanding how important love and happiness was.

I have filleted my soul wide open to you, I have told you things, done things, shared feelings with you that I never even told my dog. I am so totally comfortable with it; it is almost unbelievable to me how natural, relaxed, and free I feel when I am with you, about you, towards you. You are the eternal life-giving pill. (I hope I have the prescription with no limit on refills.)

I still get that nervous pit feeling in my chest/stomach when I am near you. I feel like I want to shout out to the world around us, as they go about their business, of my great fortune.

It is so nice to have such a warm, friendly voice say that they miss me. You make me shake with passion, love, friendship, closeness, and a desire to be needed. I am excited that I am needed, wanted and especially desired.

We keep saying we don't know how this is going to turn out because of the distance and the fact that my job requires me to travel a lot. What a HUGE, SCARY, BLACK abyss.

If you aren't sure if this is going to work out long term, as hard and painful and reflective of the pain that I once knew, before you, I will stand back and respect that. If you think that you can continue on as you were before; before my touch, taste, and feel, before my hand touched yours, before your words of love entered my ears, then you're a much stronger and courageous person than I will ever be.

If you can do none of the above, with your heart, without trying, without effort, then you have your answer and we shouldn't doubt how this is going to turn out.

I have to go away on business this weekend. I hate to be away from you, but please allow me to buy your dinner for you tonight. Just imagine that I am sitting across the table from you, looking into your beautiful eyes, longing for you, and talking about all the things we normally talk about.

You must know that you have changed my life for the better. I feel different. I realized this morning when I got out of the shower that this is the first year in years that I haven't been counting the days until I leave for my big work trip down south. This is very strange, and I know that it means something.

I have loved you from the first day I laid eyes on you. What the heck were you thinking when you wrote your number down for me? Find that answer and we will solve the question as to whether or not this will work out. This is a cycle we were meant to ride.

I think of you constantly; I dream of you nightly. I wake up thinking of you and you are the last thought before I fall asleep.

I love you, miss you, and desire to have you.

Love,

Scott

I can still love an ex as a person, regardless if the breakup was bad. I would never wish anything negative on them. It takes more energy to hate them than to wish them well.
~ Ashley Greene

Love Letter 16

Dear Kellan,

Where do I begin? You make me weak in the knees. Thanks for coming over last night! I loved the flowers, they are beautiful. These last few days with you have been amazing. Words can't begin to describe how I feel when I'm around you.

When I first saw you, across the room at Jim's surprise party, I couldn't take my eyes off of you! You are gorgeous, strong, and absolutely beautiful with your dirty blond hair and searing blue eyes. I was *not* surprised when you told me that you are in the Navy. It's clearly visible that you workout and run daily. WOW! You've definitely got a strong, and seriously sexy physique. And YES, I was very impressed with your one-handed push-ups! (Grin)

When our eyes first met, seriously Kellan, I felt like I was going to explode. We just stood there looking at each other and I felt such a pull towards you. Nothing else in that room mattered. Not Jim cutting his cake, or the band playing his favorite song. It was just you and me, and I'm so glad that you finally came over and asked me to dance.

You took my hand in yours, and led me through the crowd to the dance floor and I couldn't wait to get my arms around you. I know it sounds strange, but there is just something so familiar about you. Oh, and you smelled so good too. Wow, I just wanted to keep breathing you in. When you put your hands on my waist, it was somewhat electrifying, and I could tell you felt it too. I loved talking and getting to know you. You are so funny and you make me laugh so hard.

I'm glad that we were able to dance the night away. Having you so close was a pleasant challenge. The chemistry between us is out of control. And when you pulled back and looked into my eyes and said "I *need* to know you", I just about melted.

When they dimmed the lights and the band started playing Journey's "Don't Stop Believing", I couldn't believe how fitting the lyrics were. It's kind of funny. I just really enjoyed being so close to you. I loved how you embraced me with your strong, muscular arms, so very slowly and tightly, *after* the song had ended. And the way I could feel your breath in my hair as we danced. It was a beautiful evening that I won't be forgetting anytime soon.

And to think, I almost didn't go to Jim's retirement party at all. It was a last minute decision and now I can't imagine not knowing you. You're all I think about.

The hardest part about this for me is that you will be leaving in three days; moving far, far away to be stationed elsewhere. What am I supposed to do with that information? We've been inseparable for the last four days and now you have to go? And I have no control over it.

I know that you're needed elsewhere, but being with you just feels so right. I love how you take my face in your hands and place gentle kisses on my forehead, eyes, cheeks, and chin before you devour my mouth. Oh, how I miss you already. My body is literally aching for you.

I know you said that we can write, and call each other. And that I can come visit you. It does sound nice. Just being with you sounds nice. I like how you've planned out a visit already with amazing restaurants and such. That's really sweet and I'm so looking forward to it.

Right now, with how I feel about you, I plan on waiting forever - to the day that we can be together long-term. As long as we are together, there's no place I'd rather be.

Love,

Celia

"Letting go has never been easy, but holding on can be as difficult. Yet strength is measured not by holding on, but by letting go."
~ Len Santos

Love Letter 17

Dear Celia,

How is my pretty lady? You just left the state I've been stationed in for 11 months now. You're headed back across this vast and beautiful country we live in. But the beauty has faded on my end. It's not the same here without you. I miss you already! Watching you walk down the ramp to board your plane felt like one of the hardest things I've ever done. I didn't want you to go. Driving home without you was even worse. I felt like I was in some bad dream. I wanted to punch my steering wheel and scream. I'm surprised that I didn't get pulled over for speeding, and I don't even know why I felt the need to drive fast – I had nothing to come back to – but there was something inside of me that just wanted to slam on the gas and go as fast as I could. Escape it I guess.

I'm so glad you were able to come visit for Christmas. Best Christmas ever! We've known each other for a year and a half now and my life has been so full and rich ever since you came into it.

Today feels so dark compared to the day I picked you up at the airport... exactly 10 days ago. I know at first you thought I wasn't there, but I wanted to stand back and take you in - get a glimpse of you – for a moment I couldn't believe you were really there... looking around, looking beautiful by the way, and then when you finally noticed me standing off to the side, leaning up against the back wall, your face lit up with relief and love. I couldn't believe you were finally standing in front of me. The woman I have loved for a year now, and missed for even longer.

I'm glad you liked the spinning restaurant I took you to. It's a once in a lifetime experience that I hope you never forget. I know that I won't. I certainly won't forget feeding you the chocolate covered strawberries, or the way you licked your lips after! Man, you make me hungry. I crave you. I'm craving you right now.

I liked waking up each morning with you staring at me. And no, I didn't mind. Although I don't understand what you'd want to look at me for.

When I got back to my place I found the letter you left. Thank you. I'm looking forward to doing the word puzzle you created for me. I wonder what it says?! Thank goodness there's a secret code to direct me! You're so young at heart. It's one of the things I love about you. Everything I showed you on our mini vacation seemed to mesmerize you. You were like a kid at Disney, spinning around while taking in your surroundings, appreciating the way the trees grow here and the funny traffic signs. You are so full of life.

I have to tell you that I loved showering with you. Helping you wash your beautiful body while trying to memorize your every curve and beauty mark because I knew our time together would be short lived. You are amazing. The way you make me feel... like the only man in the world. Being with you is like Heaven on Earth, Celia.

I miss seeing your makeup and hairbrush next to the bathroom sink. I miss the smell of your freshly washed hair and silky clean body. I miss feeling you slide into bed next to me and wrap your arms around me. And yes, I even miss your cold feet! I miss kissing you. I miss seeing your heart beating wildly in your chest. I miss seeing beads of sweat form all over your body. I miss you repeating my name over and over while trying to catch your breath. I miss looking into your eyes while we make love. I miss your little giggle, and your sexy dimples when you smile. I miss your sense of humor and positive nature. Damn, I miss all of you!

My body is here thinking of you, but my heart is with you on that airplane. I hope you have a good flight home.

Missing you and loving you,

Kellan

p.s. I just finished the word puzzle. Cute and sexy! I can't wait to feel all of you again either. Xoxo

p.p.s. I'm playing for keeps where you are concerned. You were made for me.

p.p.p.s. I hope you feel the same and will wait for me.

"The scary thing about dating is that you are either going to marry that person or break up."
~ Unknown

Love Letter 18

Hi baby; love of my life,

I'm thinking of you and cannot wait to see you later! I had a wonderful time with you last night. You are amazing! You amaze me more and more every day. I'm so happy that we are together. I love you with all of my heart and soul!

I made you a CD. I know it might be corny, but these songs help put into words how I feel about you, which I'm not always the best at. Each song reminds me of you and our relationship. The first song on the CD played on the radio immediately after I first told you that I loved you. That was a special night that I will always remember.

You are so beautiful baby... inside and out! I miss you like crazy already! I appreciate you and I'm so thankful that you came into my life. I'm thankful you're in my life... forever. I'm looking forward to the years to come with you. You are the person that I want to spend the rest of my life with... and I am going to do just that!

I love you so much more than I could have ever imagined loving someone. Because of you, I finally know what love is. No one has ever made me feel the way that you have and do. I fall in love with you more and more every day. You are part of my life and I hope and want you to be forever. You are my world and I will always be here for you, through good times and bad... forever!

We will continue to learn, grow, and take on life together! You are my world, and I love you with all of my being.

I'm so looking forward to our first out-of-state getaway. This will be the first of many, for years to come. I love you more than words can express. I'm in love with you forever!

"Soul-mates are people who bring out the best in you. They are not perfect but they are always perfect for you." You are perfect for me baby and I am honored to be with you. You're my best friend. You understand me like no one else ever could. As long as I have you, no problem will ever be too big, and no day will ever be lonely. As long as I have you, I'll always have everything that I need. I feel like the luckiest guy in the world!

You are my rock. You put up with my weird mood swings. I don't know sometimes why I have them but you give me the space I need to work through them. You listen to me and always try to help me figure it out. You also put up with me when I get protective of you. It's not jealously baby, it's protectiveness. I want to protect you.

Smile baby! Somebody loves you a lot! And it's me! I love you! I want to continue to grow together, have fun, be happy, and spend our lives together, as one.

I love you with all of my heart, unconditionally, and forever.

Love,

Tim

Xoxo

"'Tis better to have loved and lost
than never to have loved at all."
~ Alfred Lord Tennyson

Love Letter 19

Hi Rose,

This is just a hey-how-ya-doing note, just to make you smile. I know how nice it is to get notes that say something, especially when it's a surprise.

You had a different sound in your voice today, not one that I think I have heard before, a little strange sounding. It had a touch of reality and change in it. Not a terminal sound, just a matter of fact sound - that a feeling of difference has happened and something inside you is allowing it to be understood. I don't know; it was still cute and erotic sounding, no surprise there. You arouse things in me like no one ever has. Even the sweet sound of your voice.

Being with you is so exhilarating. I feel young again! Alive! Like a teenage boy wanting to show off; like I did when I was 14 and went to the fair with a girl for the very first time! The excitement! The anticipation! The rollercoaster is on the way up a big hill, it is going very slow, when we get to the top it will be one hell of a ride down; it will be a quick trip, we will probably vomit several times, or wish we could. But the ride will then be soon over and we can lie down on a blanket of grass in the warm sun, listen to the birds sing happy songs, watch people as they go about their business, feed each other popcorn and ice-cream, and then fall asleep beside one another for a nice restful nap.

WOW, I almost just fell asleep at the keyboard; I am actually getting very, very, very sleepy. Yeah, I'm funny and I know it! Ha!

I was serious when I said I miss you and hate to think of you being around other men. Makes me jealous of your potential to grab whoever you'd like. Whatever, just a guy thing I guess. Thank you for letting me vent those little insecurities when they come up. It's just another thing I love about you.

Later gorgeous, I love you!

Seth

"The very essence of romance is uncertainty."
~ Oscar Wilde

Love Letter 20

Dear Natasha,

I promise to be short this time.

I must tell you again just how beautiful you looked today. You are the prettiest woman. End of that story. I just love to watch you walk, you are just so sure-footed, even that little jump you took over the puddle was cute, you glide with such beauty it just mesmerizes me.

Have I told you just how hot you look with your hair pulled back? Your gorgeous eyes just gleam above that radiant smile of yours. Every time I see you walking towards me I only wish to give you a great BIG hug and kiss. Blue is a good color on you.

I thought the article you shared with me was very interesting and really made a good point to me. Convenience, all of my previous relationships have seemed to be out of convenience. I knew this at the time and just only remembered it last night after reading that article and giving the situations some thought.

I succeeded, obviously, and I am very glad that the connection was made. There are so many examples that I can think of that must have been signs to keep looking for a different partner. I was blinded by my own self-greed. I see that now.

Being scared in a new relationship is only natural, it shows feelings and vulnerability. However, it creates an opportunity to bring yourself closer to another. It creates a lasting bond, memories.

Please know how much I love you. I adore everything about you. I plan on adoring you from now to eternity.

Lots of love,

Cameron

"Intense love does not measure, it just gives."
~ Mother Teresa

Love Letter 21

Dear Ava,

I just wanted to drop you a quick note. I must tell you how impressed I am with your ability to always have a smile on your face. You absolutely light up the darkest of rooms. I just cannot express in words how you make me feel inside when I see you smile at me. I am almost overjoyed to the point of intoxication when I see you move about the room, hear your voice, and then to see you look at me with those beautiful brown eyes, I simply melt into a handful of mushy chocolate.

You are a rare find indeed, to have you by my side is not just a treat to feed my hunger but a true opportunity to be with a great person of exceptional dignity, beauty, intelligence, trust, and friendship. You compliment the finest of jewels and rare commodities. I am honored to know you, to speak with you and to have spent special times with you. All are a true gift from a greater power. All have a special meaning, purpose and the answer to all of our past frustrations and confusions.

So what I am really trying to say is that I think you're pretty neat and I really like you a lot. I truly hope we can continue to build on our friendship so that when, and if there is more to come without being, that we will be very comfortable with each other and we can prosper with great bounty.

I think we both know that, thankfully, we have entered into a dimension that we will not be able to break free from for any amount of time. We are at the mercy of this force. I might call it Cupid, and you might call it Fate. It is probably a combination of both with a lot of love, desire, instinct, and obsession thrown in for good measure.

It hurts when we are not together during the day. It takes endurance and strength to get through these times and to get through this minefield we call life.

Know that I am ready to give you a hug every time you stand up from your desk and that I am holding your hand every time you walk to your car. When you look into the mirror, I am standing right behind you; rubbing your shoulders, scratching that itch on your back and brushing your hair.

Warm weather, clear skies, good food, cold drinks, sandy beaches, and great times lie ahead for us. Vacation is coming soon sweetheart!

So back to the present, I still think you're cute and pretty cool to hang out with, even if you are a little shy, we can work on that later.

Your best friend, and then some, I hope.

Love,

Nathan

"He is not a lover who does not love forever."
~ Euripedes

Love Letter 22

Dear Olivia,

I just want to let you know I was thinking of you. I was sorry to hear of your loss yesterday.

It is never easy to lose a member of the family, no matter what the relationship was like.

Just know that there is comfort in my arms whenever you may need it. I will always be here for you. Forever.

You can count on me, Olivia. I'm so glad that we are together and that I can be your strength when you need it. I will hold you up whenever you feel weak and unsteady. I will look out for you and care for you like no other. I love you very much.

Love,

David

"I have lost and loved and won and cried myself to the person I am today."
~ Charlotte Eriksson

Love Letter 23

Dear Monique,

I am afraid that I am pushing you; I hope you understand why. My love for you is unstoppable.

I feel like you will think that I did not hear you. I do and did, and that is what I am telling you. We can make it work, and I use the word "can" and "work" loosely, because I do not think that the actual relationship needs the work, it is the logistics that's all.

24 hours ago you were not ready to be in a committed relationship; I find it possible that today you are considering it. Talk to me about it; let me listen to your thoughts. It is okay to be a little selfish, to speak of your needs and wants. You are a beautiful human who needs love, attention, and togetherness. I am here for you; you but only need to ask and speak.

You are a fabulous person. I am so fortunate to know you, to have found you. That means something, it means a lot. It is destiny. I feel the same as I have right along, nothing has changed on my end.

Don't spend a lot of time looking into this morning. I am sorry if I was not, or did not do as you thought I should have. I did and do miss you. I would love to hold you right now. I misread you a little, that comes from not always being able to download your thoughts while you sleep. Those types of things will pass.

I love you always, don't forget that.

Anthony

*"It only takes a few seconds to say goodbye
to someone you love, but it will take the rest
of your life to forget them, because the
memory lives on forever in your heart."*
~ Unknown

Love Letter 24

Dear Claire,

I need you to be there for me

I need to be there for you

I need you to say what you have tried not to say

I need you to dig deep and listen to what you know

I need you

I am counting on you

I know you will be there for me

You looked at me this morning

Eternity in your eyes

Defiance in your words

Love in your face

Struggle in your voice

I know you

I will not fail you

I feel the power within

I feel the bond

I am seeing our future together

I do not think that I will make it without you

I think that would cause me to fail...

Will you meet me, will you join me?

Would you be with me forever?

I love you, from here to eternity

Love,

Brandon

*"Love is forever, and if it doesn't last
forever it isn't love."*
~ Dottie Kinnealy

Love Letter 25

Dear Victoria,

I do not totally agree on the newness thing. It just feels so natural and sooooo good to hear your voice. Your voice, attitude, and the smile that you project when we talk are like a sedative. You relax me, calm my tension, and make the world such a wonderful place.

When I watched you walk into the room this morning, you were such a treat. To have you close to me feels so good. You have such a calming effect on me. Even when we are not together; I cannot describe how good it feels.

I know you've made it clear that you are not ready for a serious commitment. I know you just got out of one hell of a messy relationship. I'm trying to respect your wishes on space. And I tried so hard not to send you a message yesterday, I really did try. I just needed to know you were someplace and that I might be a thought in your head for a few minutes. My greatest fear is to lose you. You are such an amazing part of my life. Every day that passes makes me realize just how much I need you in it.

I know you have told me, at least, a thousand times that you're not ready. I am trying to understand your point of view. I am being selfish and probably foolhardy. I just can't stand not being around you. My God I love you so much. I think about you almost constantly. You are the first thing that pops into my head when I wake up in the morning and the last thing I remember before I fall asleep. And while I'm asleep, I'm dreaming of you.

I have tried to envision my life without you, and all that I end up with is a black wall; a void in time that traps my thoughts.

I know that I can't force you to change your mind, and I can't force our relationship to grow faster than it is meant to. I know that this would be self-defeating, wrong and a huge failure. I am regressing to my uneducated teenage years. I want something and I can't have it. It is driving me crazy. But ever since I met you, I've known what I want. It's to be near you.

I do not have the willpower or strength right now to leave you alone. I can't keep myself from you.

We crossed paths for a reason. I hope it is so we can live the rest of our lives as one. I suppose I could be wrong; it has happened from time to time. Maybe you are just my stepping-stone to someone I have yet to meet. Perhaps you are that push I need to truly live. I've been unhappy for a long time and I'm tired of it. I am sure I have felt this for a long, long time.

I must live, I have dreams, things that I want to accomplish. When I think of my dreams, you are there with me. Please say you will move in with me?

Here I am ready and willing. I know you say you're not sure that you're ready to make such a commitment, that we may be moving too fast, but I think if you give us a chance there will be a lot of good and then great times. I know that you want to come with me. I feel it in your touch, I hear it in your voice, I see it in your eyes and I taste it when we kiss. You know.

I love you,

Toby

*"Anyone who loves in the expectation of
being loved in return is wasting their time.
Love is an untamed force.
When we try to control it, it destroys us.
When we try to imprison it, it enslaves us.
When we try to understand it, it leaves
us feeling lost and confused."
~ Paulo Coelho*

Love Letter 26

Dear Raquel,

My heart aches with your words. I have the weight of the world, it seems, sitting on my chest. I hurt because I cannot make your pain go away. I am saddened because I cannot make it better for you. It is interesting to know that when I went to bed last night at about 10, I looked at my phone and almost shut it off. But I didn't because I had this intuition that you might need to at least send me a text. I knew it was impractical for you to call so late, but I just knew that you were hurting.

Long distance relationships can and do work Raquel! I wish you'd get it out of your head that long distance relationships are bound to fail. We met online and instantly fell in love when we met in person. I felt that we needed and had to move forward. We got to a crossroad and we either stopped cold or turned the page. It was a calculated risk of sorts, but I felt in my heart that it was the right thing to do. I heard your words and knew that I needed to take the lead. I hope that I chose correct, not so much for me but for you. I was sent into your life for a reason. You may be hurting and struggling right now. And I'm sorry for that, but it's for a reason. You just have not been able to see it yet. I think it has been around for a while and that you have been ignoring it. Being with you is natural. We've created a connection between us that was destined to happen. You know it. It's not the physical but the emotional element that we created that is so special.

More importantly, you can trust me! I have no intentions, never have, never will, of hurting you, physically, mentally, or emotionally. You are acting this way and have these immense feelings because you not only love me but also want a more committed relationship with me. I know exactly how you feel, 100%. So many people have successful long-distance relationships, and we will too! We can make this work. Look at people who are in the military and have to be apart for long periods of time. They don't just break-up or stop seeing each other just because they can't see each other every night. They don't quit! Don't quit on me!

This pain and uncertainty that you feel only makes you stronger in the end; it will make our lives and relationship so much stronger. There will be a trust and honesty that you will never understand until we start to live it. When two people have lived the same sadness, hopelessness; the same desperate feelings, it makes each other realize that they have been blessed with a gift of true love.

Neither one of us has ever been in a relationship that has ever given us true love. We have both just been puppets in a show, being controlled by the present and by what was expected, so it seems.

Stop questioning our relationship. Stop saying that it won't work. Stop saying that I'm not listening to you. You need to look at yourself in the mirror and tell yourself the truth. Say it 21 times a day for 7 days. This will allow your conscious to catch up with your subconscious. Your real mind has already decided for you; just realize all of your past relationships were only a temporary fix to get you to the point in your life where you found me. Roll with it; stop fighting it or you will end up permanently scarred.

I have in some regards misjudged you. You are more fragile and tender than I once thought. You are extremely sweet and sincere and sensitive.

I was really trying to be relaxed with all of the unknowns. I have faith.

My thoughts are always with you and about what would you think, how would you feel, how would you react?

I am over the past issues. I thought back then that there was no way I could move on, and then I figured there must be a reason but could not fathom what it could be. I know now, it was to build a relationship and a trust that will hold up through anything that gets thrown at you or us. I believe in us that much, I trust you that much, and I love you that much.

Nobody else has ever taken care of my needs like you do! No one! No one compares to you. I love how I feel in your presence. I love that we can have intelligent conversations. I love your positivity. I love your innocence and fragility. You are the one for me. You complete me. The sooner you understand that this is reality, the way it was meant to be, believe it, understand it, the better you will feel and any doubts that you have will subside.

I will always be here for you if you let life take over and stop fighting with your internal compass. Long distance relationships work for many people and we can make it work for us too. I know it won't be easy, but I feel that we are meant to be together no matter what obstacles are thrown our way!

It broke my heart when you told me that you felt your heart break in your chest with my words. That you felt sick inside. That your bones hurt from the heartache. That there was so much "dis-ease" going on within your soul. You said it wouldn't happen again and that I would never hurt you again. I said never say never. I meant never say never to us being together. I am sorry if I hurt you. I'm sorry if you no longer trust me. I do not know what else to say. I know that you are in love with me; I truly believe this is a fact. I know that we will be together for years to come. Don't shake your head; this is a sign of defiance. It means you need to start from the top again.

Know that I love you, I always have. That is why this is so easy for me. I told you, that night when you walked towards me, I absolutely knew at that moment everything you said, have done, written, touched, sensed, felt; it is all real. I have been great from that moment on. I believe in you. You are strong, and instead of focusing on what could go wrong, you need to try to enjoy the present.

Time will heal the uncertainty and doubts. And with it our love will prosper and spill over. Everything will be better because of our ability to see through the uncertainty. It's called life.

I am a lucky guy because I have seen the truth, and I am going to move forward with what is right for me. You are what is right for me. I know this to be true. I am what is right for you, and you know this to be true also.

I've been waiting for someone like you, and there's no way I'm going to let you go. Not just because of distance! There are planes, buses, trains, and automobiles, and I'll be damned if I'm going to let a few states come between our love.

Do this, every time you get that unsure feeling in your stomach, close your eyes and pretend that the pain is being caused by my head laying on your tummy and that I have fallen asleep. The pain in your head is because I have kept you laughing and smiling too long. The tears rolling down your cheeks because I put too many onions in the dinner I cooked for you. The pain in your heart, because I am sitting on your chest because you won't tell me where you hid the remote control to the TV! The discomfort you feel from your body aching, because of our continued lovemaking. That made me smile.

You are an amazing, beautiful person. I am so fortunate. You have direction and love. You have a good heart and a good soul. How I got so fortunate, I will never know, but I'm not going to question it. I am going to trust how I feel about you. We can get through the distance. We can plan trips and vacations together. I know you are trying to look at the big picture and the future, and maybe even having kids someday, but we will figure that out as we go.

I wish I could give you a much-needed hug and hold. I wish I could smell your scent of love and life. I wish I could taste your lips of happiness. I wish I could be with you right now.

Stop being mad, sad, and unsure; it stops NOW.

I love you, I miss you, I need you, and I want to be with you. I need your love and life. I will give you all of the same in return. You are my friend, my partner, my lover, and my world. We are as one.

With Love, Ian

"Falling in love is like jumping off a really tall building. Your brain tells you it is not a good idea, but your heart tells you, you can fly."
~ Unknown

Love Letter 27

October 1985

"My Name is Mandy"

I think we met on a circle waltz,

In the Spring of "eighty – five".

I remember your style of dancing,

Made me feel great, and so much alive!

But summer has past unto fall,

And we meet once more, at the C & J Hall.

From that night on, it was plain to see,

I was good for you and you were great for me.

That I'm beginning to like you,

To want you close both night and day.

And the memories of those kisses,

I'm a fool to stay away!

So now I'm able to date you.

It's the distance that keeps us apart.

I remember about our yesterdays,

And the dancing gave us our start.

Now I think about tomorrow,

No more pain and no more sorrow.

And yet the eyes might shed a tear,

To hold you close and have you near!

Thank God we have tomorrow,

Each is different in its own way.

How great it is we have our health,

And watch our children as they play.

More and more I want you near me,

More and more you're on my mind.

I really believe that I'm a winner,

And a girl like you is hard to find!

I hold your hand when we go riding,

Or squeeze your leg when you are near.

So many things I like about you,

And the "thank-you's" are great to hear!

Love,

Jon

"To be fond of dancing was a certain step towards falling in love."
~ Jane Austen

Love Letter 28

November 1985

Not long ago when hunting,

I thought about you gal.

And the minutes seemed like hours,

You might say – I missed my pal.

But tonight I'm warm and cozy,

Yes! I'm with my girl tonight.

And I chase her while she house works,

But later on, I'll hold her tight.

She's all woman, she's a lover,

She's the one that I want most.

And when we go out dancing,

You can hear the people boast!

It's just great to watch you guys,

We love to watch you dance!

And backing up the months,

That's just how I got my chance!

We love to go out dancing,

I get my exercise that way.

For some, it seems a struggle,

For me, I love it; another way to play...

Our music is strictly country,

It's no good for a broken heart.

Let's all think about tomorrow,

Smiling seems like a good way to start!!!

Love,

Jon

"What we have once enjoyed and deeply loved we can never lose, for all that we love deeply becomes a part of us."
~ Helen Keller

Love Letter 29

April 1, 1986

Dear Mandy,

It is time to write my weekly letter, and I'm feeling great about it! How great it was to see you Sunday night and dance many dances with you! On my way home, I was listening to WPOR and smiled to some of the good waltzes and songs we have shared together. Only a short time before we were doing, what we like to do so well... I love to see you excited; your bright eyes and smiling face. Talking and being with you was wonderful. I want for, so much, but don't know how to make it happen. I'm just a dreamer and do too much thinking, and no action. But, that's the way I've always been. I try to smile and make everybody happy even when I'm hurting on the inside and time passes -.

And there you were, at the singles Sunday dance and my heart started pounding! I know you can do better, than with me, but it doesn't stop my wanting and loving you.

I have done the wash and now the clothes are in the dryer. When they are dry, I'm leaving to have lunch with Frank. He got home yesterday and I talked with him this morning on the phone.

Thank you for the phone call last night. My e.s.p. was working and I was hoping to hear from you. I know you must think of me a lot because I sure do, you.

Please remember when you're cooking, that I love eating and love your tasty cooking and I want to be in your life. I'm only a phone call away. I came to you when there were others in my life, now let me come to you with love in my heart.

You're a wonderful person and one heck of a special mother – you're not some crazy mixed up person. If your heart begs to call me, then do it. Happiness is important!

Lovingly yours,

xo Jon xo

"Falling in love consists merely in uncorking the imagination and bottling the common sense."
~ Helen Rowland

Love Letter 30

May 10, 1986

5:40 p.m.

Happy Mother's Day

Nobody has told me about you,

But the people are many, that care.

And I beg you to look my direction,

Open your eyes, be brave, say "I dare".

Be happy and the world smiles with you,

Live music and a good country song!

For so long, I've wanted your likeness,

And without you, the day is so long.

Today is our day for "Mothers",

And you are so special of all.

For I, am nothing without you,

But with you, I walk straight and tall.

Yes, today, I want to be with you,

No more games, for it comes from the heart.

And you can be proud of your children,

You have done so well, on your part!

Xo Love, Jon xo

"Bad things do happen; how I respond to them defines my character and the quality of my life. I can choose to sit in perpetual sad-ness, immobilized by the gravity of my loss, or I can choose to rise from the pain and treasure the most precious gift I have – life itself."
~ Walter Anderson

Love Letter 31

December 16, 1987

Dear Mandy!

My words and what I had prepared myself to say when I called you and after having a drink were not the same? I picked the #1000 out of my head, I thought it sounded good!

I've wanted very much to talk to you and have asked you out to dinner twice now.

You haven't seen or heard the last of me yet because I love and miss you very much. I know you have been through "hell and high water", and I enjoyed doing what little I could for you.

Please get yourself a little something with the money enclosed (maybe a pair of dancing shoes). My heart says the world, but my pocketbook says $50.00. And the savings bonds are for the kids so they'll remember me. I love you all....

Just me, with love!

xo Jon

P.S. Merry Christmas and a great New Year, Okay?!

"First best is falling in love. Second best is being in love. Least best is falling out of love. But any of it is better than never having been in love at all."
~ Maya Angelou

LOVE INSIGHTS

Love doesn't just sit there, like a stone; it has to be made,
like bread, remade all the time, made new."
~ Ursula K. LeGuin

READ ON FOR IMPORTANT love insights that will help you see things from a different perspective. These love insights were submitted by those who have experienced breakups, divorces, and by those who have maintained healthy, long-term relationships and marriages. Some insights may be difficult to read while others may get you excited and hopeful. Everyone is different so take what resonates with you, and let everything else go. Even if you find just a few new ideas to move forward with, you will find that your relationships can thrive and be better than ever before.

Love; it can be confusing, yet wonderful. Unfortunately, many failed relationships happen because the people in them haven't been taught the proper skills needed to have, and maintain successful relationships. However, we can't blame others for not teaching us how to love and be loved because people can't teach what they haven't learned themselves; things they don't even know or haven't experienced. But, the good news is, we can stop and break the cycle for our family, and for future generations to come.

The first step in creating the love that you want is to be open to the fact that you don't have all of the answers. There is no way that we can have all of the answers when it comes to love and relationships. We are all learning and growing as we go along and each relationship is unique. Once you accept that you do not have all the answers, then, and only then, can you begin to move forward with an open mind in search of your truth. With an open mind, you will be able to accept that if something isn't working, maybe it was a false belief that needs to be changed. With this awareness, you can live a limitless life, and will make progress towards moving in the direction of your dreams. The direction your inner-being is leading you towards.

For some reason, we tend to hold tight to the beliefs that have been instilled in us. Beliefs, I might add, that have been instilled in us by others. They are not even our own beliefs! We are learning things from people who are in unhealthy and dysfunctional relationships themselves. We are learning things from dramatic television shows and Hollywood movies. Why then, do we cling so desperately to them? It's like we automatically believe what we've been taught; therefore, we fight for that belief, even if what we've been taught might not be everything we want it to be; even when it doesn't feel right for us.

You may have been brought up in a family with a single mother where you heard her say - on more than one occasion - that all men are liars and cheats. This belief was instilled in you, but it doesn't make it true. It's a false belief.

You may have been brought up in a family with parents who fought, argued, and belittled each other all of the time, where you witnessed marriage being a sad and unhappy union. This belief was instilled in you, but it doesn't make it true. It's a false belief.

You may have been brought up in a family without a father figure where you didn't receive male affection, while your friends and neighbors did, and you were left feeling alone, insecure, unworthy, and unloved. This belief was instilled in you, but it doesn't make it true. It's a false belief.

You may have been brought up in a family with parents who abused cigarettes, alcohol, and drugs; where it was the norm to see the people you looked up to smoking and drinking. Maybe you grew up witnessing a lot of unhealthy choices, and the belief was instilled in you that this is what grown-ups do. But it's a false belief and doesn't make it true.

You may have grown up surrounded by teenagers who were having sex and thinking nothing of it; where being surrounded by this type of behavior and peer pressure made you wonder if you should do it too. More of your friends, than not, were talking about being promiscuous, and it made you think this must be the norm, but it's a false belief and doesn't make it true.

You may have grown up seeing your parents, your friend's parents, aunts and uncles, neighbors, teachers, and others giving up easily on their relationships and getting divorced, and remarried; sometimes more than three or four times. You may have seen people breaking their promises, and leaving their spouses for someone else. The belief that this is okay may have been instilled in you, but it's a false belief and doesn't make it true. Love is not self-serving and does not hurt others.

You may have grown up hearing that you should "sew your wild oats" before settling down; that you should "shop (aka sleep) around" before tying the knot. This is a false belief, which can only lead to heartache, sexually transmitted diseases, and unplanned pregnancies. There are plenty of couples that learn the skills needed to maintain a healthy relationship with their first love... because they have been taught what to look for. There are a lot of people who grow in good character, where good morals are instilled in them from a young age; therefore, they look for those qualities in others and don't settle for anything less.

We need to open our minds, and start to think for ourselves! We need to start taking control of our own lives! We need to start asking ourselves important questions, and then listen to the still-small voice within for the answer.

We are not in kindergarten anymore. We no longer need

to believe everything that we are told. We no longer need to believe everything we witness or experience as being the only way.

If something doesn't feel right within, stop and ask yourself if what you are experiencing might not be the only way. Look for solutions. Look for other options.

If you're uncomfortable with something that someone is doing or saying, then that is an indicator that you need to move in a different direction.

Life can be glorious when we learn that love is what we make it. What are you waiting for? Go forth and create the life you've always longed for. It is within your grasp and only your grasp. No one else can live your life for you. No one else can think, act, do, be, or love for you either. No one can create better habits for you. It's your choice, and you get to go where you want by taking one step – in the right direction – at a time.

Get ready to take the wheel of your life! Roll the window down, smell the fresh new air as the warm breeze blows through your hair. Experience certainty and confidence as you punch in the destination of your choice into the GPS, and trust that it will lead you directly where you choose to go.

1. Acceptance

IF YOU HAVE RECENTLY EXPERIENCED a breakup, the first thing you need to do is breathe. Accept that you will be upset. This is a natural response to a break-up. A break-up is a big change, and change can be difficult.

If your significant other has told you that they no longer want to be with you, you need to maintain your dignity. You shouldn't beg, freak-out, go crazy, stalk, throw things, disrespect, or act desperate. Do not take it personal. I know this is easier said than done, but you can do it. When someone decides they don't want you in their life anymore, it has everything to do with them, and nothing to do with you. Most likely they are looking for happiness and love outside of themselves. They have inner work to do. You can love, support, and try to help others, but you cannot change them. You are an amazing soul; a unique individual who needs to trust that the Divine Source must have better plans in mind for you.

You should, however, maintain control, hold your head

high, and be thankful for the experience; while having faith that everything always works out. It's okay to cry, that's natural when dealing with a loss of any kind, but if someone no longer wants to remain in a committed relationship with you that, my friend, is their loss.

And remember, actions speak louder than words. Trust yourself. Trust your intuition. If someone says that they want to be with you, but come Friday and Saturday night they would rather be elsewhere, you may want to rethink the situation. They may not be being true to their word.

We need to learn to accept the behavior of others by not only their words but by their actions as well.

SUBMITTED LOVE INSIGHTS ON ACCEPTANCE:

I was in a dysfunctional relationship for 15 years. I don't know why, but I just couldn't accept that things weren't going well. I kept hoping that they would get better. My boyfriend kept being dishonest, and I felt that I should forgive him over and over because I loved him. I wanted to believe what he was telling me, but it seemed like he didn't have the truth inside of him. He would say one thing but do another. He was very distant, but he said he loved me, and although I wanted to believe it, I still didn't trust him. I started looking at his call records and texts messages and there was nothing out of the ordinary. But his behavior said something totally different. After several months, I learned that he had purchased a track phone that he was hiding from me and that he was practically living with someone else when we weren't together. He told me he was staying with his mom. I was heartbroken but still wanted to believe him. Looking back, I was so foolish, but I finally learned that I needed to stop believing his words, and start believing his actions. ~ Ann

One evening, after crying for several hours, I finally turned to God. My husband had been unfaithful on more than one occasion, and my heart hurt so bad, I didn't know what to do. I remember praying. I pleaded with God to take the pain and hurt away. Immediately I felt a relief. The pain wasn't 100% gone, but it was definitely better. I knew God was there with me and that he'd help me get through it. I forgave my husband, and we tried counseling, and although nothing was changing, I did not want to get divorced. I came from a split family and I swore I would never do that to my children. I also promised to stay married for better or for worse. I kept trying to make it work, and my husband and I kept falling further and further apart. I tried to be the best wife I could, and my husband didn't seem to notice. At one point I told myself that I would just stick it out and wait for him to come to me, but after a while, I felt as though the light is my soul was becoming dimmer and dimmer. I wondered if separating and being alone might be better than being sad all of the time. We started arguing in front of the kids, and eventually I had to accept that things were not going to change. Accepting that my marriage was over was not easy, but I trusted God's plan. Looking back, we went about getting married the wrong way. We weren't taught, first of all, what qualities to look for in a potential partner, and secondly, how to cultivate a successful marriage. We really thought we could just fall in love and wing it – even though we both came from split families. We fell in love very quickly, moved in together before we really even knew each other, became somewhat obsessed with each other, became pregnant, and got married. Not a recipe for a successful marriage to start out with. I asked God to forgive me for breaking my promise and moved forward striving to always do the right thing. I slip up from time to time, but try to make things right quickly, and now, 20 years later, I can tell you that God has blessed me abundantly. I can't imagine my life being any other way. ~ Mary

"Acceptance of what has happened is the first step to overcoming the consequences of any misfortune." ~ William James

"Trust in the Lord with all thine heart; and lean not unto thine own understanding. In all thy ways acknowledge him, and he shall direct thy path." ~ Proverbs 3:5-6

2. Responsibility

WE ARE NOT GOING TO GET anywhere in our relationships if we do not take full responsibility for the part we play in them. Whether we are putting up with being mistreated, or we are the one who is doing the mistreating. Whether we are the one doing the forgiving, or we are the one starting the arguments. Whether we are the one apologizing, or we are the one blaming. Whether we are the one causing unnecessary problems and drama, or we are the one finding solutions.

We are always responsible for at least 50% of everything. I know that is hard for some people to understand, but in any relationship, there are two parts.

If you are the one being mistreated, you are responsible for calming articulating your needs, wants, and desires. If you see sincere improvement, then it's your responsibility to express your gratitude and appreciation for those changes. If nothing changes, then maybe it's time you take responsibility for your happiness, and respect yourself enough to walk away.

If you get into an argument with a loved one, do you have to be right, or can you accept differences in opinion?

If something is not going well, can you take responsibility to make the necessary changes to make it better?

SUBMITTED LOVE INSIGHTS ON RESPONSIBILITY:

It took a long time for me to accept responsibility for my miserable life. I was a single mother, working two jobs and still not making ends meet. My kids were distancing themselves from me. I was missing their important games and school activities. I was alone and sad.

Just eleven months prior, I had been a stay-at-home mom in a good marriage, but I felt like something was missing so I started talking more and more with a man I knew. At first our emails were just friendly banter, but soon they became flirtatious. We decided to meet for coffee, then dinner, then for nightcaps at his family's secluded camp. I was making more and more excuses for being away. I also started finding all sorts of things about my husband that I didn't like. He didn't pay enough attention to me. He didn't take out the trash quickly enough. He didn't take the kids to their doctor's appointments. He didn't make me laugh like he use to. He didn't spend enough time brushing his teeth. He didn't wash his hands frequently enough. He was the reason I was doing what I was doing! I justified my behavior over and over. And, of course, I fell in love with my male friend with whom I was spending all of my spare time with and sleeping with regularly. He was all I thought about, and he was married too. I'm not proud of the choices I made, but at the time, I was selfish and blind.

I got divorced, got a job, moved into my own apartment and hoped my male friend would leave his wife as well. But he didn't.

My bad, dishonest, selfish choices had led me from a happy, secure life, in which I didn't appreciate, to being a single mom, lonely, poor, and missing out on my children's lives and activities. What had I done? How could I be so selfish? How could I be so blind? All of this misery... because I had allowed myself to slip into something that wasn't right in the first place. All of this emptiness, because I was dishonest with myself and so many others... others I professed to love. Love is not being dishonest to the ones you love. Ever. I couldn't believe how my life had turned out.

Until one day, I was so depressed that I cried out to the Universe. Why are you doing this to me?! Why does my life suck so much? Why me? I felt immediate conviction in my heart. It hit me like a ton of bricks. It was all my fault. I had gone about it the wrong way. I had strayed in more ways than one. I had strayed from my husband, from God, and from my moral obligations. I felt like I had high morals, but obviously, I didn't. I lacked honesty, integrity, and loyalty in this situation even though I thought I had good excuses for doing what I was doing. I was blaming others for MY bad behavior.

I sensed that I needed to humble myself and apologize and come clean for all of my wrongdoings. And that's what I did. I apologized to my ex-husband, to my children, and to God. It wasn't easy admitting what horrible choices I had made. Looking back, I couldn't even believe I had done the things I had. Those choices had severe consequences, but today was a new day and I was committed to moving forward with a new and stronger spirit.

After a while, my ex-husband finally forgave me. He was very angry at first. My children were very upset with me too, but eventually, they thanked me for telling them the truth. And God forgave me and gave me another chance.

My life started getting better. I received a big promotion at work and was able to quit my second job. My new position allowed me to set my schedule so that I no longer missed my children's activities. And I started attending church regularly, where I met the man of my dreams. Taking responsibility takes courage, but it's well worth it.
~ Sherry

"I felt ashamed for what I had done. I don't have any excuses. I did what I did. I take full responsibility for myself and my actions. I wouldn't pawn this off on

anybody. I'm sorry it happened. And I hurt people."
~ Louie Anderson

"We are made wise not by the recollection of our past, but by the responsibility for our future."
~ George Bernard Shaw

3. Build up your character. Who do you want to be?

START ASKING YOURSELF SOME important questions. Who do you want to be?! What kind of person do you want to be? Decide who you want to be, and start being it. It's really that simple. Start acting the part and you WILL become it. It is important that we continually strive to better ourselves, to improve, to learn and grow.

Do you want to be strong and confident or cowardly and insecure?

Do you want to be someone who only thinks only of themselves or do you want to be someone who gives and loves as much and often as you can?

Do you want to be a giver or a taker?

Do you want to help others or let opportunities to help others slip by?

Do you want to be a grumpy, miserable person, or do you want to be friendly, kind, loving, caring, and joyous?

Do you want to live a mediocre life, or do you want to live

out your dreams and live an outstanding life?

Do you want to be a complainer, or do you want to be an appreciator?

Do you want to be depressed, or do you want to be happy?

Do you want to be dramatic, or do you want to be calm and peaceful?

Do you want to be a good, faithful, loyal and loving partner? Or do you want to be lazy and allow yourself to fall into negative habits because that's easier?

Do you want to be someone who has high morals and high standards, or as someone who can't be trusted?

Do you want to be a jealous person or a trusting person? And please don't say that you can't help being jealous. I know that jealousy seems like an automatic response because of the actions of others, but it's not. It's a choice. When you find yourself starting to feel jealous about something, stop yourself by becoming present. Get in the present moment, and ask yourself why you are feeling the way you do. It might stem from a past relationship, or a past family matter, or from a soap opera that you watched yesterday or years before. Your insecurity could be coming from someplace stored deep down in your subconscious mind that wasn't put there by you. It wasn't a deliberate choice, but it's there. It was put there by outside circumstances. Either way, take a deep breath and realize that you have a choice in this moment. You can get jealous, in which nothing good can come. Jealousy will negatively affect your body, and behavior. Or you can DECIDE to come from a place of love. Love is trusting, patience, calm, kind, is not jealous, and does not blame or accuse.

You can change who you are with your deeds and actions. You can change your habits and become the person you want to be! You can become an amazing wife or husband. You can become a terrific mother or father, daughter or son. You can become a great employer or employee. You can become who you want to be, by taking action. It's not always easy to break bad habits, but it is possible! And successful people prove it every day. Every moment is a new opportunity to start fresh.

SUBMITTED LOVE INSIGHTS ON CHARACTER:

I couldn't wait to get married. I just knew it would be wonderful and blissful. A couple years into my first marriage, I became somewhat lazy. I hate to admit it now, but looking back, that's exactly what happened. My husband would come home, and I'd be sitting on the couch watching my favorite television show... and I'd stay there all night. I'd hear him in the kitchen doing the dishes, but I couldn't seem to tear myself away from my show or the commercials even. I could sense that my husband was starting to resent me as he tidied and cleaned up around me. But we were married, and it was comfortable and I didn't think anything would ever change. We were married... in good times and bad; in lazy times and even lazier times. My husband asked if I'd get up and help him pick up, and I'd playfully whine that I didn't feel like it. And this continued for months. It didn't feel good not helping out, and I didn't even like living in the pigpen-like conditions we had somehow grown into. But sitting on the couch and getting lost in a television show or movie was easier and far more fun than cleaning. But it wasn't rewarding at all, in fact, I felt bad about it. Yet I still continued to do it because it didn't require any effort at all.

Eventually, my husband fell out of love with me, and even though I apologized, it was too late. I'm sure there were other little things that contributed to our failed marriage, but this one weighs heavy on my heart. How hard would it have been to get up and pick up after myself? How hard would it have been to shut the television off? Not hard at all. I think that had I taken 20 to 30 minutes a day to help out, I could've saved my relationship. But I learned that lesson a little too late.

I now know that self-discipline is one of the greatest rewards we can give ourselves. When we are disciplined in one area, we will automatically become disciplined in other areas of our lives and then it becomes easier and easier, and the benefits of such character-building traits are truly unending. ~ Anna

"I'm am better than I was yesterday, but not as good as I will be tomorrow. I am in competition with no one. I have no desire to play the game of being better than anyone. I'm simply trying to be better than the person I was yesterday." ~ Unknown

"Good character is more to be praised than outstanding talent. Most talents are to some extent a gift. Good character, by contrast, is not given to us. We have to build it piece by piece by thought, choice, courage and determination." ~ John Luther

4. Love Is What You Make It

LOVE IS SO POWERFUL. It can make all things better. It can make the darkest day brighter. When two people fall in love, there's generally nothing that can bring them down. New love is a natural high. It doesn't matter if you're tired and didn't get enough sleep. It doesn't matter if someone cuts you off in traffic. It doesn't matter if bill collectors are calling you day and night. New love makes you feel like you're on top of the world no matter what is going on around you. You find yourself smiling and giggling without a complaint in the world. Oh, and yes, love is blind. This saying is most popular and so well-known for a reason. Why is it that when we are in love, we are blinded from any wrongdoing on our partner's part? If they forget to call... no problem! If they forget to pick up something on the grocery list... no problem! If they forget to put the toothpaste cap back on... no problem! Oh, the honeymoon phase is so joyful and blissful. So what happens? Why do things change? Why do the rose colored glasses fade? Why does time hinder this amazing feeling? It's called the after-a-while-human-take-for-granted-ness. That's my terminology for it anyway. And yes, I've fallen prey to this awful diagnosis. We all can, and do, but we don't have to. It's a choice.

If we can learn to love our spouses without expectations, we will experience the most blissful relationship ever. We instinctively love certain things without expectation; our children, our pets, and even certain foods and activities. What do we tend to do when we love without expectation? We easily and effortlessly love. That's what we do. We adore our children and pets, and while doing so, we express and experience that pure love so much, that we end up loving them even more; if that makes sense. That love builds and grows even stronger.

What do we do when our children sleep? We stare at them and say things like:

Oh, how beautiful!

I can't believe how much I love this precious child.

Thank you, God for this amazing blessing!

I could stare and marvel at this creature forever!

What a beautiful birthmark.

What beautiful little fingers and toes.

Oh, let me kiss your precious forehead.

I could hold your hand forever.

I could hold you forever.

I love you more and more every day.

Love is the most precious gift and because of you, I know it!

What do we say when our children mess up? We love them and say things like:

That's okay, everything will be okay. I love you.

I'm here for you always. I'd do anything for you.

You're an amazing person.

I will always see the good in you.

I support you always.

I forgive you.

And it's basically the same way with the pets we love with all of our hearts. We cuddle with them, and say things like Oh, you're so cute! I can't get enough of your cuteness, thanks for always being here for me, thanks for being loyal, thanks for listening, thanks for always being happy and excited to see me, oh, you're so adorable, and fun, and you make me smile, etc., etc.

These thoughts and feelings generate more of the same.

This effortless love seems to come naturally with our children, and pets, and relatives, but it's the way all of our love relationships should be. Unfortunately, pride and the feeling of separateness can sometimes get in the way. We can make our love relationships stronger and build on them, with our actions, and thoughts. But it remains our responsibility.

SUBMITTED LOVE INSIGHTS ON LOVE IS WHAT YOU MAKE IT:

I've been married three times, and I'm not proud of it. When my third marriage started heading down the same path as my previous two, I knew that something had to change! I finally came to the conclusion that I may be the common denominator in these failed relationships. But, believe me, it took me a long time to get to that point. I wanted to blame everyone and everything else. It was not easy and was a long process before I finally admitted and took responsibility for my part in these unsatisfying relationships.

My third husband was starting to do things that did not please me. And probably if I started to list off the things he did, you might end up agreeing with me. Isn't that what we tend to do at times? Our emotions get the best of us, even if we don't know the whole story. We are supportive beings, so when someone is feeling neglected, we want to stand up for them. Here's the thing. It's just one person's perception, and may not even be the entire truth.

Anyway, after being married to my third husband for five years, he started to ignore me, my wants, and my desires. At least, that's how I saw it. And I got more and more frustrated, and more and more distant, which, of course, only made matters worse. After a while, and many months of justifying my disappointment and aggravation, I told a very wise friend that I had had enough! I was going to ask for a divorce.

My friend suggested that before I file for divorce, I try just one simple thing. She told me that I needed to take responsibility for my part of the relationship. I scoffed at the idea even before I heard it. And a part of me wanted to walk out on her. I didn't feel as though she was hearing me. Hadn't she heard me complaining for the past year?! Why wasn't she supporting me and my decision?! But I had known this wise friend for years, and I trusted her. She had a great marriage and a beautifully healthy family life. So I let my anger, and the red face I felt, subside, and I took a deep breath and listened.

She suggested that first I pray, and second, that I only think positive things about my husband for 30 days. She told me that when a negative thought popped into my head about my husband that I needed to change it immediately and replace it with a positive one. She told me to write positive statements about my husband on an index card and to carry it around with me and to read it as many times as I could throughout the day. She also suggested that when I lay in bed, while my husband slept, that I should first thank God, and second, think loving things before I fell asleep, such as: I love my husband so much. I'm so thankful to hear my husband breathing next to me. I love my husband so much. I'm so grateful that I get to share this moment with my husband. I love my husband so much. I love, love, love, my husband! I love his ears and his bald head. My husband is the very best! I love my husband so much.

I told her that I'd give it my best shot, not thinking anything would change. She wanted me to be accountable, so she printed off a month calendar for me and told me to cross off each day so that we'd be sure I had followed through with it for the entire month. Amazingly enough, around the 15th day, something inside me changed. I sincerely fell in love with my husband all over again! It was a miracle it seemed! And my husband sensed the change as well. Around the 20th day we were making love like we had in the very beginning of our marriage! We couldn't get enough of each other. My husband couldn't wait to get home at night, and I couldn't wait either! We started enjoying each other's company and conversation again! We've now been married for 10 years, and our relationship just keeps getting better and better! ~ Danielle

"We've got this gift of love, but love is like a precious plant. You can't just accept it and leave it in the cupboard or just think it's going to get on by itself. You've got to keep watering it. You've got to really look after it and nurture it." ~ John Lennon

5. The Three F's

FORGIVENESS, FAITHFULNESS, and Friendship. In order to have a successful relationship, you have to learn how to forgive. Nobody is perfect. We all make mistakes. We all learn differently. We all have different childhoods. We all have different insecurities. We all have different needs and wants. We all have different ideas of how things should be. What is extremely important to one person may not be to another. And that is okay. Yes, it is good to have similar likes, and beliefs, but there is no possible way for two people to think exactly alike. And that's the beauty of a relationship. Things are always different. It's about give and take. It's about compromise, and being open-minded enough to look at things differently. The Bible shares incredibly wisdom on forgiveness. It says that we should forgive endlessly. You forgive, until the person you are forgiving has a change of heart. They will learn from your example. This is not to say that you should put up with being treated badly because you shouldn't. But learning how to forgive others is a freeing experience, and it is a powerful act of love. Forgiveness is giving others the freedom to make mistakes. Which we all do. When you forgive, you are "erasing" it. You are wiping the slate clean. This doesn't mean you won't ever recall the difficult situation that needed forgiveness, but it does mean that you will remind yourself that you've let it go and that it's time to move on from it. Real love holds no records of wrongs. Remind yourself of this when needed, and choose to focus on the future not the past. Choose to focus on the good. Choose to deliberately choose what thoughts you will think. It takes practice, but we can choose what thoughts we think. If a negative thought comes floating through seemingly automatically, tell it where to go, and replace it with a happy, feel good thought. It's so freeing to learn how to master your own mind. You are the master of your soul. Take charge and don't just allow autopilot to take you to places that do not serve you and your soul.

Having a forgiving heart takes practice. Practice is the act of continually doing something over and over until you master it. Keep at it. Learning to forgive everyone and everything will free you... from all sorts of negative internal reactions.

Besides being faithful, and having a loyal character, you have to have faith in your relationship, as well. Faith is believing in things unseen. You can't think about what could go wrong, or focus on problems or issues. You shouldn't ignore your problems, but you also shouldn't let them outweigh all the good that makes your relationship what it is. Try to stay in a place of faith that things are always working out for the good of your relationship. Faith is huge. You can't have a doubtful - quit during the hard times mentality. There is a solution to every problem, so trust that. If two people really and truly want to be together, then they will find solutions, take full responsibility, and act on those solutions. And they will enjoy, and have fun, doing so. Love doesn't quit, it endures.

Friendship is also an important part of any relationship. Your partner should be a best friend, therefore, you need to treat them like a friend. You need to show them love, respect, kindness and be there for them in good times and bad. You need to make time for them, and take their thoughts and feelings into consideration, always. The most successful relationships are those that have formed a sincere and deep friendship.

SUBMITTED LOVE INSIGHTS ON THE THREE F'S:

When I was asked to write a little on forgiveness, I immediately knew what I would write about. Four years ago, I forgave my husband for cheating on me. During that time, and in some of my darkest hours and sadness, so many of my "friends" told me that I should leave him. "Dump him!", "You don't deserve that!", "Once a cheater, always a cheater.", "Kick him to the curb." They'd say. Thankfully I grew up in a family that gave second chances. We weren't expected to be perfect. We learned that people make mistakes. Believe me, forgiving my husband was one of the hardest things I've ever done. The woman he cheated with lived in the same town as us and frequented many of the same places that we did. But I believed that he was sincerely sorry, I wasn't ready to throw away all that we had together, and I was willing to give him another chance. If his actions didn't reflect his words, then I would reconsider. Thankfully, he followed through, and not just for the first few months, but he hasn't stopped since. He spoils me, treats me like never before, and we are now best friends. It's hard to admit, but his affair strengthened our relationship and made it better than it had ever been before. I had to learn how to forgive both my husband and the woman who lived two streets over. I had to learn how to hold my head high in town while others were whispering. I had to learn how to hold onto my faith and know that it didn't matter what anyone else thought about me, my husband, or our life together. I had to learn that true friends will support you even if you have differences of opinions. ~ Ruth

As I sit and write this, my boyfriend is working late. AGAIN. My mind wants to think the worst. Why is that? All of these doubtful thoughts come to mind. Where is he really?

Is he meeting someone? He works an hour from home, how would I ever know what he is really doing? Should I try to track his location by his phone? Is he meeting someone? What does she look like? I bet she doesn't have sweatpants on, or a baby on her hip like I do right now? NO NO NO! I have to put these thoughts to bed. Is my husband in bed with someone else right now? NO NO NO! I get to choose what I think about. I'm an adult and I know this. I will choose to think only on positive things. The love I have for my family. My beautiful cuddly cat. My cute loyal and loving dog. My friends. My hobbies. I choose to have fun regardless of what my boyfriend is doing. I'm going to trust what he tells me because that's the decision I've made. Period. We have a good relationship and just because I've recently heard of other break-ups and affairs, that doesn't mean anything. Those outside forces do not have to carry into my relationship. I also know of several very successful and loving relationships. My insecurities from the past do not need to rear their ugly heads. I need to have faith and stand firm in it, and that is just what I will do. ~ Beth

"Now faith is the substance of things hoped for, the evidence of things not seen." ~ Hebrews 11:1

"For we walk by faith, not by sight" ~ 2 Corinthians 5:7

6. The Golden Rule

TREAT OTHERS THE WAY you would like to be treated.

Do you want your significant other to be giving, kind, and respectful? Then be that way. Do you want your significant other to be easy-going, fun, and light-hearted? Then be that way. Do you want your significant other to bring you a surprise gift from time to time? Then give them a gift from time to time. Do you want your significant other to be loyal, forgiving, and honest? Then be that way yourself. Do you want your significant other to put the phone down, and look you in the eye while talking to you? Then put your phone away, and look into their eyes, while you are with them.

If you ever find yourself wishing your significant other would do 'this or that'? Do 'this or that' for them.

"You must be the change you want to see in the world." ~ Mahatma Gandhi

SUBMITTED LOVE INSIGHTS ON THE GOLDEN RULE:

My wife and I were married for five years when I started slacking I guess. Looking back, I can see it much clearer now, but at the time, I felt as though life owed me. I was a responsible husband and a father to beautiful 3-year-old daughter, with another on the way. I worked two jobs, and my wife worked full-time as well and we still were financially strapped. The one night I had off was Friday nights, therefore, I wanted to go out with my guy friends, naturally. The bars would close at 1 but we'd always find a place to party afterward, so I wouldn't get home until 3 or 4 a.m. at times. I worked as a bartender other nights, and basically the same thing would happen. My pregnant wife would be up waiting for me and I could always tell she had been crying. She knew the bars closed at 1 but never asked where I had been for the last 2 or 3 hours. I felt bad, but I felt as though I deserved this little bit of freedom, even though I knew she had to get up in 2 hours to go work her day job.

My wife was beautiful and I know if roles were reversed I would NOT like her behaving as I was. She'd always try to get me to see it the other way around, but I'd always tell her that I couldn't relate to that scenario because I knew she wouldn't do that. She was better than me.

It wasn't until after our divorce, and then another failed marriage, that I finally started to see the true meaning behind truly treating others the way you'd like to be treated.

If we did this in all of our relations and in all of our interactions with others life would be so much better.

I hope everyone learns this lesson. If people learn to truly treat others the way they would like to be treated, there would be no reason to hate or envy another. Our souls would be free. ~ Jim

"Practicing the Golden Rule is not a sacrifice; it is an investment." ~ Unknown

"We have committed the Golden Rule to memory; let us now commit it to life." ~ Edwin Markham

7. List it.

THIS IS SO SIMPLE that anyone can do it. I have four suggestions for lists that you should start right away.

The first list that you should start compiling is a list of things that make you laugh out loud. Anytime something makes you laugh, really laugh, jot it down. You will enjoy putting this together and anytime you are feeling down, just pull out your list and it will immediately make you feel better. You won't be able to keep yourself from smiling. I think this list is so important to keep with you at all times.

The second list should be a list of all the things you love about your partner. If there are 9 things that you currently can't stand about your partner and only one thing that you like, then only focus on that *one* thing you like. Over time, list everything that you like about your partner. Do you like that they took out the trash? Do you like that they hugged you when you needed it? What qualities do you love about them? What do their friends and family like about them? Jot all of these down and ONLY focus on these things. Like attracts like, and you will get more of what you focus on.

The third list should be a list of all the things you love about yourself. This is probably the hardest list for people to complete. For some reason loving ourselves is one of the biggest and hardest challenges that we face, yet it is clearly one of the most important. You cannot love others if you don't first learn to love yourself. Fortunately, with practice, we are all capable of learning new things. And you will learn to love yourself if you follow this simple step. Over time, write down things you love about yourself. Even if it's as simple as a task you completed. Did you make it to an appointment on time? Good for you! Jot it down. You have to start somewhere and making it to appointments on time is an accomplishment! Once you start learning how to love yourself as a friend would, you will start to truly love yourself unconditionally. That is the goal. You will learn to love everything about the unique you that you are. We are all made different so that we can fit together with those around us. I truly believe that we are all one. Each of us has our own strengths and weaknesses because that benefits the oneness that we are.

The fourth list will be a prayer list. If you don't want to call it a prayer list, then call it an intention list. I can't begin to tell you the evidence I started seeing once I started to implement using my prayer list every morning and night. I went to a journaling class one evening and the instructor told us that he felt led to start a prayer list. That still-small inner voice said to him "I want you to experience the power of prayer." So he started writing down the names of people he felt led to pray for. Some were strangers so he didn't even have a name for them, but he'd write down a description so he knew who the intended prayer was for. He said although he didn't know everyone on the list, those that he did know, about 75% of them, he saw clear evidence of positive changes in their lives.

So I started my own prayer list. On one side I have those close to me who I want to pray for. My husband, children, parents, etc. And on the other side, I have strangers I might come across, and those who I normally would never even consider praying for. Those who I have ill feelings towards. Those I don't get along with. I say a quick prayer over each name in the morning, and a prayer for each person before I go to bed at night. I don't say a long, drawn prayer out for each person. I trust that God knows that person's desire. I ask God to send the Holy Spirit to them and to bless them. To let God's will be done for that person. For that person to see themselves as God sees them. And I cannot begin to tell you how rewarding this prayer list has been for me. It feels so freeing praying for those I have a hard time understanding. But I pray for them regardless, and over time, it's as if this huge chain, that has been wrapped around my soul for so long, is slowing being loosened. Break the chains, God! It's been an amazing experience and I have seen positive (I'm talking incredible!) evidence in the lives of those I have been praying for. It's been awesome. Try it for yourself.

SUBMITTED LOVE INSIGHTS ON LISTS:

Loving myself had been the hardest thing for me to do in my life. I am 50 years old, and I think I'm finally starting to get it. I always felt like I was confident enough. I took care of my health and body. I tried to walk tall and appear confident. But I always, always caught myself dissing myself in my head. I'd say 'Suzie, look at that nose of yours.' Or 'Suzie, from the side view your neck looks like a turkey neck. Suzie, you might as well not even go out because you look like crap. Suzi, you don't cook dinners for your family like the other women at your church do, you suck! Why does your husband even stay with you?'

It was almost constant. And I hated it, which just gave me another reason to dislike myself. I hated that I thought thoughts that I hated thinking!

Sage told me to start a Love Me List. At first, I laughed out loud, right? As if! I really didn't have much that I loved about myself. Although I was thin, I was super flabby, almost everywhere. I loved my kids but always felt that I wasn't doing enough for them. The list goes on and on. I told Sage that I didn't think I'd have much to put on the list.

She told me to start with simple things. As simple as getting the kids to school, and brushing my teeth. It sounded so silly, but she said those things are definitely accomplishments. We, as humans, tend to judge things by size. I thought those things were too little accomplishments and not worthy to be put on my list, but Sage said an accomplishment is an accomplishment. She said to get braver over time and that it'd get easier with this process. The goal was to eventually love everything about myself. Because ultimately we are perfect in the Creator's eyes. It's been a long journey but I am starting to accept myself fully. It feels wonderful. I love my list and myself! I recommend this to everyone. ~ Suzie

"Love yourself first and everything else falls into line. You really have to love yourself to get anything done in this world." ~ Lucille Ball

"In everything give thanks: for this is the will of God concerning you." ~ 1 Thessalonians 5:18

"Be grateful for what you have now. As you begin to think about all the things in your life you are grateful for, you will be amazed at the never-ending thoughts that come back to you of more things to be grateful for. You have to make a start, and then the law of attraction will receive those grateful thoughts and give you more just like them." ~ Rhonda Byrne

8. New Experiences

WHY ARE NEW RELATIONSHIPS always exciting? When relationships are new everything about that relationship is new, therefore, everything is exciting! Human nature tends to drive us into routines. Eventually, new things become comfortable and then over time we tend to get bored. We start to slack off. We start to take things for granted. We don't laugh or giggle as much anymore. Taking out the trash isn't as fun as it once was. Seriously, in the beginning, taking out the trash with your new lover was exciting. You don't care what you do as long as you are together! When we are in the first stages of a relationship with someone, everything our significant other does makes us laugh. We wouldn't imagine bitching or complaining. Over time, more and more things slowly start to annoy us and we feel freer to express our discontent. We should not allow ourselves to get to this stage

Relationships that seems to last, most often have a

freshness to them. Here are a few ideas of how you can instill new experiences into your long term relationships so that you can keep them fresh and exciting.

Set up date nights to places you've never been. Do this once a week, or once a month to start. Explore new towns, new restaurants, and new places. Just drive, be spontaneous, see where the road takes you and then find a place to stop to get a bite to eat. Try out different beaches, campsites, movie theaters, parks, bike trails, etc. Let a travel agent arrange for a mini-vacation for you to a place you've never been. Travel agents are totally worth it, and most of the time their fees are included in your price. I've used a travel agent for years now and when I compare, her prices are always cheaper than if I did all of the planning myself. And travel agents know what they are doing. Find a travel agent, tell her the amount you'd like to spend, and let her help plan your annual vacations. Create a list of new places you'd like to explore. Most of the time, the very state we live in has many attractions we've never experienced. Do a little research and start having fun with this. You can't help but feel excited when you are in a new atmosphere with your significant other. It time to create new experiences, and let your life explode with excitement and adventure.

SUBMITTED LOVE INSIGHTS ON NEW EXPERIENCES:

When Sage told me her idea of creating new experiences,

I liked the sound of it. My wife and I have been married for 15 years and I will admit that our relationship had become quite boring. It's not that we didn't love each other anymore, because we did, more than ever. We have a great relationship, but come Friday night, we'd tend to look at each other and not know what to do with ourselves... so the same thing usually ended up happening. We'd try to find a good movie on Netflix, which usually took forever, and then we'd go to bed early. We used to go out dancing, laugh all night long, and then come home to a wild night of love-making. After 15 years, we had definitely found ourselves in a rut.

So upon Sage's request, I immediately went to the task of finding new experiences for me and my wife to explore. I sat down and researched all of the local attractions in my areas. I was surprised to learn that not even a half a mile from us there was over 100 acres of biking and hiking trails. Only 30 minutes from our home there were hundreds of restaurants, several were waterfront. I found boat tours and booze cruises. The list of opportunities seemed endless and I was excited. I started a list. We would try to do one new thing a week. Hiking was free so we started there. The scenery was amazing, the fresh air was intoxicating, and it felt great on our bodies. We had great conversations and many laughs that first day. The second week, I planned a romantic dinner on the water. We sat next to a cozy fireplace that overlooked many beautiful boats. The food was delicious, the wine was even better, and we ended up staying at a local hotel across the street. It was spontaneous and fun. We didn't have a change of clothes so we just made due with what we had. It was something we would've done when we were first dating. Since then we've gone to many music concerts, movies, museums, clubs, parks, etc. We like to go biking and canoeing. We've had a lot of fun. And Sage was right, one of our favorite things to do is to just drive. When we find a place to eat that feels right, we trust that feeling and stop. We see so many new things this way. The next thing I want to do is plan a cruise. I think now that we are in the swing of it, this will be even more exciting. Thank you, Sage, for all of your input and advice. My marriage has improved significantly and I wouldn't want it any other way! ~ Jack

"The joy of life comes from our encounters with new experiences, and hence there is no greater joy than to have an endlessly changing horizon, for each day to have a new and different sun." ~ Christopher McCandless

9. Karma/Law of Attraction

THIS IS ONE OF MY FAVORITE subjects because I see the evidence of it so often. What goes around comes around. Like attracts like. You are what you think. You get what you give. You cannot avoid any of these simple facts.

We all vibrate. We are energy vibrating. Our energy vibrates at different levels and we control this with our feelings and emotions. We also control our feelings and emotions with our thoughts. For the most part, we have been taught to believe that we have no control over any of this, but it's simply not true. With a little practice, we can unlearn all of the negative programming that has unconsciously made its way into our brains.

Here's the basic concept. What you do, comes back to you. Like a boomerang. It's just the way it works. So try to remember this when you are going about your day. You can research this yourself, but Love, for instance, is a high vibration. When you are resonating from this level, you will attract similar experiences that are on that same wavelength. Hate is a very low vibration. So if you feel hate towards something or someone, you unknowingly, or now knowingly, will attract similar low vibration experiences and feelings to you. Such as jealousy, depression, envy, etc. Things of this nature will be offered to you, automatically, without hesitation, by the Universe. You can play with this and test it for yourself. If you talk negative about or even have negative feelings about someone, you will attract low vibration frequencies to you. If you cheat on or lie to someone you will attract similar low vibrational things and experiences towards you. If you feel happy, and loving towards someone or something, then more happy and joyful things will be brought into your experience effortlessly. It's just the way it works. Once you become aware of this, you will start to recognize it.

The Bible tells us to think on only thoughts that are pure, just, fair, and good. I don't think this is a coincidence. Our thoughts will become our reality. We can't just pretend to be happy and expect good things to come our way. We have to deliberately be happy, by choosing our thoughts.

Another thing that has come to my attention on this subject is in regards to our family pets. You cannot talk in a loving, cheerful voice to your cat or dog and not get a positive response from them. Like attracts like. You talk lovingly, they can't help but respond. My cat purrs the minute I start talking lovingly to her, and with my dog, she instantly starts wagging her tail when I talk in a joyful tone to her. We are vibrational beings.

One time I was watching a sad movie. When I started to feel myself choking up, I knew that I should just shut it off right then and there, because I have learned, at this stage in my life, that, no, I do not really 'need a good cry'. Watching something, and allowing it to bring me down, literally, does not benefit me in any way. So, I was watching this movie, and I started to choke up, but I continued watching. Within minutes, I was sobbing uncontrollably, and by the end of the movie I was crying for three entirely different reasons that had absolutely nothing to do with the movie. I had attracted three similar vibrations to myself during that time. Thankfully, I was aware of it. If I hadn't been I may have cried all night long. Instead, I chose to think on thoughts that brought me joy and I slowly started to raise my vibration back up to where I wanted it. Where I wanted it! You see, it's a choice.

SUBMITTED LOVE INSIGHTS ON KARMA / LAW OF ATTRACTION:

When Sage asked me to write a little something on the subject of Karma, I automatically knew what I was going to write about. I've thought about this for years because I've seen it with my own eyes. I will start with a man I know personally. He had an affair on his first wife. She caught him in their bed with another woman. They had young children and she ended up having to raise them by herself. The man ended up marrying his mistress, and they had children together. His second wife ended up partying often without him and cheating on him even more often than that. He was devastated, and they ended up going through a nasty divorce. His wife built a wall between him and his children and he basically missed out on their childhoods. He remarried and his third wife had an affair on him as well. I believe that we all make mistakes, yes, but if we don't come clean, ask for forgiveness, and do everything in our power to turn it around-to make things right then we will get what we have given ten-fold. I know a woman who had an affair on her husband of 20 years with a co-worker. She left her husband for this new man. The new man eventually left her for another co-worker! She begged her husband to take her back, but he had already moved on and was committed to his new lady. He believed in commitment. She has been alone and has lived with this regret, for over 30 years now. Another situation is of a friend of mine. He was married with a young son. He had an affair with a co-worker and eventually got divorced and married the co-worker. His new wife didn't get along well with his little 2-year-old son, so he ended up signing his rights over to another man. He let another man adopt his son. He relinquished all parenting rights, including having any kind of relationship with him. He and his second wife were miserable together and ended up getting divorced as well. So now he has no wife and no son. I could go on and on with stories such as this. When you do the right thing, things will work out for you. It's a law of the universe. ~ Tina

"There's a natural law of karma that vindictive people, who go out of their way to hurt others, will end up broke and alone." ~ Sylvester Stallone

"Problems or successes, they all are the results of our own actions. Karma. The philosophy of action is that no one else is the giver of peace or happiness. One's own karma, one's own actions are responsible to come to bring either happiness or success or whatever." ~ Maharishi Mahesh Yogi

10. What's Your Cause?

THIS IS WHERE YOU HAVE a choice. You always have a choice; you just don't always realize it. Until right now, that is! Here in this very moment. You, my dear, have a choice. What do you want? What do you *really* want? Sometimes we think we know what we want, and we really believe it, but our actions prove otherwise. We do things to self-sabotage what we think it is that we want. It might be because of some deep rooted seed that was planted inside of us when we were younger, or a disbelief that we are worthy and deserve the best. But today is a new day! We are going to decide right now what we want, and we are going to move forward towards it. What is your cause? That's the key question. The most important question that you need to ask yourself and decide on. Once you answer that question, then you can move in the right direction and be more aware of your thoughts and actions if you are not following through with your decision. I'm not sure if you've ever recognized, before, that whatever cause a person wants to believe in, stand for or represents, they WILL find evidence to support their cause. Everyone does this. But if you really look, you can and will find evidence on BOTH sides of any topic. This is where your decision comes in. Your choice is very valuable because it will determine the evidence you will find to support your cause. It starts in your mind, and if you're not careful, you will find evidence to support what you are focused on. Whether it's what you want or not.

Here are a few quick examples.

Have you ever known a person who is in debt, but convinces themselves that they NEED to get a loan for a new car because their current vehicle is falling apart, needs a new muffler, has a lot of miles on it, etc.? The reasons (excuses) go on and on. This person has convinced themselves, therefore, they will justify their cause and find reasons to support it. Nothing anyone else says will convince them that maybe they should buy a used car instead, save up so that they can pay cash for another vehicle, or get a second opinion about their current car.

Have you ever been around a person who had a good marriage, but after being pursued by an attractive co-worker, became so focused on all of the negative things about their marriage that that was all they saw? No matter what you said or did to remind them of how good they had it, nothing could convince them otherwise. And slowly their 22-year marriage crumbled because they forgot what their true values were.

They found evidence to support the attractive co-worker's pursuits, and slowly lost everything because of it.

What you focus on, good or bad, positive or negative, you will find evidence to support it. So be very clear on what you want. If you want your relationship or marriage to work out, you have to stop focusing on the negative things that you don't like about it, because your mind will justify that "cause". You can't say that you want your marriage to work and be the best it has ever been, yet focus on things about your marriage that you don't like. It does not work that way. Plain and simple. Your brain can not decipher between what you say you want, and what you are thinking or are focused on. Remember whatever cause you choose, you will find evidence to support it. So get clear. If you want an awesome relationship with your partner, then find evidence to support your cause. Stop yourself every time you have a negative, low vibration thought, because that is not the cause you have chosen. And you will only attract more of the same to yourself.

If I want to have a great relationship with my husband, then I cannot complain to my girlfriends that my husband drives me crazy because he doesn't put the toilet seat down, or because he forgot my birthday once again. I have to stop myself because this does not justify my cause. My cause is to have an amazing marriage with the man I fell in love with 16 years ago. That is my cause. I have to focus on what I love about my husband and only talk with him and God about my frustrations. I have to think of things to praise him about while I'm talking about him with my friends. I once believed that doing this was being dishonest; that the reality of my situation was that he was driving me crazy, but I quickly learned that I create my reality and I get to choose what to focus on. Since then I have experienced a freedom like never before. I create my reality and I'm going to be deliberate and create a good life. One that I want.

SUBMITTED LOVE INSIGHTS ON WHAT'S YOUR CAUSE:

This is hard for me to admit, but it's the truth, and I now see it. I was foolishly fooled years ago. Fooled by my own pride and ego, I guess. I was married to my high school sweetheart. We had three beautiful children together. And we had a good marriage. We laughed, we loved our children, we knew everything about each other, and we had a great sex life. We fit in every way. 18 years of good, and then a woman at my work started flirting with me. She was 15 years younger than me and very attractive. She started giving me these looks that lasted longer than the normal looks people give each other, attached to a sensual smile. She started to brush up against me on her way past me. We had to work together, therefore, we had each other's cell phone numbers. She started texting me jokes and they made me laugh. When she started sending me nude photos of herself, I started to delete them right away. I found myself getting anxious when I'd get any text messages because I didn't want my wife to see them. Of course, the man in me wanted to look at these beautiful photos of this woman, and man did it ever feed my ego. Someone as young and beautiful as she was, attracted to me?!

After a few weeks of this, I told her that she needed to stop. I told her that as flattering as it was, I was married and knew that it was only exciting because it was new and forbidden, really. She disagreed. She said she just wanted to be good friends. That she knew we were brought into each other's lives for a reason. I was one of her best friends and I was helping her through some tough times.

So we started meeting each other in the cafeteria and we always laughed. We were always giddy and silly in each other's presence. She'd briefly place her hand onto mine as we talked. We even had inside jokes going that only the two of us shared. We'd text each other songs that reminded us of each other. I started to confess problems I thought I was having in my marriage. My wife would complain because of something, and I'd justify my misery because of it. My wife would have a bad day at work, and I wouldn't want to hear it.

When I found myself buying this other woman a Christmas gift, I justified it with just being a gift for a co-worker. It was a bracelet and I paid cash for it so that my wife wouldn't find out.

Everything I did, I found justification for. It seems absolutely ridiculous now.

I remember meeting with a relative of mine. I asked, "what do you think of my marriage?" This relative told me that she loved to see my spouse and I laugh at family outings, that she thought we had an amazing relationship that many people would aspire to have. Then she surprised me when she said she felt that I sometimes she felt that I was rude to my wife. I'd rudely joke that I thought she was eating too much, or laugh at her when I probably shouldn't. This surprised me. Me? Not treating my spouse to the best of my ability? That was nonsense! It was my wife, who wasn't treating me as she should.

When my wife complained of a headache and failed to do any of the household chores or family laundry over the weekend, leaving me without any clothes to wear, I was so frustrated I had to get out of the house! I texted my co-worker, and she told me to stop over. We shared our first kiss that day, along with a lot more. She willingly gave herself to me and although it felt amazing – I felt like a teenager without a care in the world - that was the beginning of a nightmare for me. She became obsessive, texted me constantly, and wouldn't leave me alone at work.

Although not religious at all, I remember feeling that she was leading me down a path of destruction. I clearly remember thinking this is a road to the Devil. I knew there was nothing good that could come from this, but I couldn't seem to stop myself from seeing her.

Long story short, my wife found out about us. And we decided to try to make our marriage work. I knew this was the best thing for all involved. My co-worker disagreed and wouldn't let up on contacting me. She'd even stop at my wife's work and harass her.

As hard as I tried, I couldn't break the chains this woman had on me, and I was eventually convinced that my wife was a complete bag. Something that never crossed my mind before this woman entered my life. My wife and I eventually divorced, and five years later, after years of dysfunction, fights, drugs, alcohol, and drama, the woman who is 15 years younger than me decided she wanted someone younger.

What was I thinking? To this day, I don't know. But I believe we can learn from other people's mistakes. Life is too short to experience all of the crap decisions we humans seem to make from time to time. We need to be open about our flaws and weaknesses so that others can learn from our situations. ~ Tony

"Finally, brethren, whatsoever things are true, whatsoever things are honest, whatsoever things are just, whatsoever things are pure, whatsoever things are lovely, whatsoever things are of good report; if there be

any virtue, and if there be any praise, think on these things." ~ Philippians 4:8

11. Habits

YOU HAVE TO CREATE habits that will benefit the life you want. Ask yourself what kind of life you want? Then ask yourself what you need to do to accomplish such a life? You will never discover what you truly want until you learn to talk to yourself. By talk to yourself, I mean start asking yourself some important questions. If you had a job or project that you were assigned to at work, you would need to ask your higher-up some questions, do some research to find the answers, and then follow through to complete it. You were assigned this life.

Do you want to be healthy? Then what habits do you need to incorporate into your lifestyle?

Do you want to start your own business? Then what steps do you need to take to get started?

Do you want to be a straight A student? Then what habits, actions, and behaviors do you need to start instilling into your everyday life?

Do you want to grow your relationship with our Divine Creator? Then start forming habits to support this. Whether that is getting up early to read the word, or signing up for a Bible study, or buying a workbook online to help you.

Do you want to be a positive person and think on only pure, righteous things? Then what do you need to do to become such a person? Maybe correct yourself every time you have a negative thought. Eventually, you will create a better way of thinking.

Do you want to be a good friend? First, describe what that looks like to you and then start forming habits so that you can succeed.

Do you want to be a good wife, husband, significant other? Then what can you do right now to move in the right direction to accomplish this?

Habits are nothing but continued actions. You can create new habits. Nothing can change in your life until you change your habits. The good news is that you can do anything that you want to - with will and determination. Get started today! Form habits that will benefit you and your life. All things are possible!

SUBMITTED LOVE INSIGHTS ON HABITS:

I recently created a new in my life. It's been exhilarating and powerful! It did not happen overnight. It took time and patience and a sort of gentleness with myself. The first thing that noticed about myself, and wanted to change, was that I'd often find myself having negative and judgmental thoughts. They'd spring up out of nowhere it seemed. I knew this was not a Godly attribute so I asked God to please help me with it. Once I asked it seemed like this floodgate opened and I really started to become aware of my thinking. That same day while waiting for my child to get out of school, I noticed that almost every kid, coming out of the school, had a cellphone in their hands. I immediately had a judgmental thought pop into my head. Look at all these kids focused on their cellphones! They are not even appreciating the nature or other human beings around them! Parents are so dumb to allow this type of behavior. What is this world coming to? I quickly realized what was happening and apologized to the Universe for this thought behavior that I did not want to be a part of me. I said "I'm sorry. Please forgive me, and please bless all of these kids. Let them feel your presence and love, and become all that you know they can be." Not even two seconds later, a teenage girl walked by in a very, very short miniskirt. Judgmental and opinionated thoughts began rearing their little heads almost like they knew she was coming. Just look at her! A bit slutty wouldn't you say? I can practically see her underwear! I hope she doesn't need to bend over anytime soon. Does she think she's at some night club or something? This is a high school for goodness sakes! Then my inner being immediately felt convicted. These were not thoughts I was proud of. I didn't want to be a judgmental, critical snob. Who was I to even think such things? I didn't know anything about these people I was thinking such negative things about. I said "I'm sorry. Please forgive me. And please bless that young lady whom you love dearly, God. She is yours, just as I am, and you love and want the best for all of us. You commanded us to love one another and that is what I am striving for." I experienced thoughts such as these four times in a five-minute span while I waited for my son. And then on the way home when I saw two teenagers groping each other and a pregnant woman smoking. "I'm sorry. Please forgive me. You love all. Please wrap your arms around them and bless them." This went on for about two weeks until I finally starting finding myself automatically wanting to bless everyone who came into my experience! Strangers on the street, people passing by, parents who were yelling at their kids in the grocery store, and those who were not. I wanted to bless everyone here and there and everywhere. With constant practice, my thought habits have completely been transformed. It's been so freeing! And lovely. ~ Jennifer

After complaining to Sage about my eating habits, she told me to ask myself what I really want. She said I had to be clear and that it wouldn't hurt to write it down. When I started to tell her that I seemed to have no self-control and that I really wanted to make healthier choices when it came to eating, she stopped me in my tracks. She said "You don't have to tell me what you want. This is between you and you." She also said that I didn't have to write out some expansive report, it could be simple. So that's what I did. I wrote down what I wanted and what I needed to do to accomplish it. My idea of health was to exercise 30 minutes a day and to eat only fruits, vegetables, along with a few grains, beans and rice 6 days a week, which would leave the 7th day open for a few sweet treats. There it was. Plain and simple. So that's just what I did. Sage was right, it was between me and me. I've been living a healthier lifestyle for over two months now, and can't believe I use to buy into the excuse that I had no self-control. I'm so grateful for such simple, yet helpful advice. It's made all the difference in my life. ~ Brenda

"The people you surround yourself with influence your behaviors, so choose friends who have healthy habits". ~ Dan Buettner

"I never could have done what I have done without the habits of punctuality, order, and diligence, without the determination to concentrate myself on one subject at a time." ~ Charles Dickens

AFTERWORD

"You must unlearn what you have been programmed to believe since birth. That software no longer serves you if you want to live in a world where all things are possible." ~ Jacqueline E. Purcell

The intention of this book was to provoke thought and action; to empower you on your journey, and to remind you of your strength. When you make it a habit to incorporate positive changes into your life, one day at a time, you will reap many benefits. Live in the present, and appreciate each day while moving forward toward your dreams and goals... one baby step at a time. We are meant to love, have fun, and dream big!

We lead by example. Here's to raising our children to have good morals, and to be of high character.

12 Things Happy People Do Differently

1. Express gratitude

2. Cultivate optimism

3. Avoid over-thinking and social comparison

4. Practice acts of kindness

5. Nurture social relationships

6. Develop strategies for coping

7. Learn to forgive

8. Increase flow experiences

9. Savor life's joys

10. Commit to your goals

11. Practice spirituality

12. Take care of your body

About Sage Wilcox

Sage lives in New England with her husband of 16 years, children, cat and dog. She inspires to be a Life Coach and enjoys giving advice to her friends and family on love and relationships. She also enjoys studying human behavior, reading, writing, being outdoors, and spending time with her loved ones. She enjoys her women's groups and being active in current groups through her church. These groups usually consist of 9 to 12-week courses using different books and study guides for a more in-depth learning of the Bible and scripture. She inspires to help young people recognize how valuable and precious they are, which she hopes will create self-love, self-confidence, and self-worth.

Please visit her website at:

http://sagewilcox.wix.com/books

Disclaimer

The purpose of this book is for entertainment purposes only. This book is designed to provide information and motivation to our readers. The content of each article, letter, or insight is the sole expression and opinion of its author, and not necessarily that of the publisher. The letters contained in this book are from contributors and are the contributor's recollections of their experiences. This is a work based on opinions, recollections, and true events, however, names, characters, businesses, places, and incidents are either the products of the authors' imaginations or used in a fictitious manner. Any resemblance to actual persons, living or dead, businesses, companies, events, locales, or actual events is entirely coincidental. This book is not intended nor is it implied to be a substitute for professional medical advice, and any medical advice and any medical information contained in this book is not intended to be diagnostic or treatment in any way. The author and publisher are not engaged in rendering medical, psychological, legal, or any other professional services. If medical, psychological or other expert assistance is required, please talk to your physician and locate the services of a competent professional. The author and publisher shall have neither liability nor responsibility to any person or entity with respect to any loss or damage caused, or alleged to have been caused, directly or indirectly, by the information contained in this book. Neither the publisher nor the individual author(s) shall be liable for any physical, psychological, emotional, financial, or commercial damages, including, but not limited to, special, incidental, consequential or other damages. Our views and rights are the same: You are responsible for your own choices, actions, and results. If you do not wish to be bound by the above, you may return this book along with a copy of the receipt to the publisher for a full refund.